HANDBOOK OF AUDUBON PRINTS

Handbook
of
Audubon
Prints

by
LOIS ELMER BANNON
and TAYLOR CLARK

PELICAN PUBLISHING COMPANY  GRETNA 1985

Library of Congress Cataloging in Publication Data

Bannon, Lois.
   Handbook of Audubon prints.

   Bibliography: p.
   Includes index.
   1. Audubon, John James, 1785-1851. 2. Birds in
art. 3. Prints, American—Collectors and collecting.
4. Prints—19th century—United States—Collectors
and collecting. 5. Ornithologists—United States—
Biography. 6. Artists—United States—Biography.
I. Clark, Taylor, joint author. II. Title.
QL31.A9B36   599'.092'4   79-1319
ISBN: 0-88289-202-9

Manufactured in the United States of America
Published by Pelican Publishing Company, Inc.
1101 Monroe Street, Gretna, Louisiana 70053
Designed by Oscar Richard

To Jane and Lew

Contents

LIST OF ILLUSTRATIONS

Acknowledgments

It was almost twelve years ago that Dr. Robert Engass, who was chairman of the Louisiana State University Fine Arts Department, suggested that I narrow my art history thesis idea to one phase of John James Audubon's work for a book. At that time I began my detailed research and my long friendship with Taylor Clark, who has generously shared his vast knowledge of Audubon with me and who asked me to collaborate with him on this book.

The Louisiana State University Library Staff has been extremely helpful to both Taylor Clark and me, especially Evangeline Lynch and Mary Jane Kahao. I am additionally grateful to Mrs. Kahao for allowing me to use some of her own Audubon research.

Other institutions whose staffs have given generously of their time and services are the Library of Congress, the Boston Museum of Fine Arts, the Carnegie Library in Pittsburgh, the Boston Athenaeum, the Houghton Library at Harvard, the Louisiana State Museum in New Orleans, the Charleston Library Society, the Cincinnati Historical Society, and the New York Historical Society, whose former curator, Caroline Scoon, was most helpful.

Personal acknowledgments are due Marion Carson of Philadelphia, who allowed me to use her personal library;

9

Mrs. Henry Hoffstot, Jr., who made research contacts for me in Pennsylvania; Vaughn Glasgow, who did research for me in Pennsylvania; Edward H. Dwight, Director of the Munson-Williams-Proctor Institute and an authority on Audubon; Eric Hardy, British ornithologist who helped me in England and sent information from that country; Peter Manigault of Charleston, who sent information about Maria Martin; Mrs. Francis Coffin of Charleston, who is a descendant of the Reverend John Bachman; the late Isaac Sprague, Jr., grandson of Isaac Sprague; Tom Scott of Mexico; and Dr. and Mrs. M. L. Griswald of New Jersey. In addition to Robert Engass, other art historians who assisted me were Robert Day, James Reeve, Helen Bullock, and Mr. and Mrs. Martin Weisendanger.

Any book about Audubon would be difficult to write without information available in the late Francis Hobart Herrick's biography of Audubon. Alice Ford's well-researched biography of Audubon has also been of great assistance. Waldemar Fries' *The Double Elephant Folio* is an invaluable source of information.

Special thanks go to Mrs. Thomas Smylie, who edited my part of the book, and to my husband, Lewis Bannon, who aided me in my research, especially when we traveled to other states and other countries.

Lois Elmer Bannon

Preface

"Why did you tell me this was an original Audubon lithograph?" asked our friend. "My aunt who knows all about Audubon said it was probably by his son and lithographed by somebody named Bowen." We took from the shelf a large book about *The Quadrupeds of North America* and a small book about original prints.

"Are the small animal prints by Audubon; who was Bachman? Did he draw some of the animals too?" he asked. We pulled another book from the shelf and handed it to him.

"How can I tell a Bien from a Havell?" More questions and more explanations followed. Finally, we gave him a bibliography that we hoped would satiate his curiosity.

This experience was not an isolated one. In fact, both of us have been through something similar so many times that we decided to put into a book the research we have each been gathering the past several years.

Never before has a single book presenting concise information about all of the prints of John James Audubon been available to students of Audubon and collectors of his famous prints. As we pursued our own research, we found numerous books about Audubon's fascinating life as well as many books and articles about the large engravings for *The*

Birds of America. However, finding detailed information concerning all of Audubon's bird and animal prints required reading published and unpublished articles, diaries, letters, and other books relating to the artist-naturalist's works and examining many of the prints themselves. We began to understand why there has been much confusion and misinformation about them.

The information we have obtained is presented for the reader who is interested primarily in Audubon's prints. This book is not a biography, but rather an explanation of the work and a brief discussion of the various persons involved in producing the prints. It is designed as a reference handbook so that the reader can look up specific information about a single print or an edition of prints. The first two parts by Lois Elmer Bannon are devoted to background information, and the third by Taylor Clark is devoted to evaluating the individual prints.

The various editions are often referred to by their size, the terms being elephant (or double-elephant), imperial folio and octavo or royal octavo. These are publishers' terms for the size of the book or folio in which the prints were bound, and are not consistent measurements. The measurement in inches is given at the beginning of each chapter concerning an edition. Definitions of engraving, aquatint, etching, lithography, and chromolithography are not included in the book. The novice to the field of fine prints can find information about these techniques in most encyclopedias.

This book is for those persons seeking detailed information about Audubon's prints, and should give the reader some appreciation of the monumental task Audubon undertook to create and publish them.

Introduction

John James Audubon was the natural son of Jean Audubon, a French naval officer, sea merchant, and planter, and Jeanne Rabine, a French woman he met on a voyage to Santo Domingo.[1] He was born at Aux Cayes, Santo Domingo, now Haiti, in 1785. These are the accepted facts about his birth in spite of persistent rumors that he was the lost Dauphin, the son of Louis XVI and Marie Antoinette, or that his mother was a mulatto, or that he was born in Louisiana, a story used by him and his father to aid his departure from France and avoid conscription into the French army.[2] At the age of six years he had arrived in France, where he was lovingly reared by his father and his father's legal wife. Throughout his youth he preferred rambling the countryside and drawing birds to pursuing his academic and naval studies.

When he was eighteen years old, he was sent to America to help supervise his father's plantation, Mill Grove, in Pennsylvania, where his consuming interest in American birds matched his interest in French birds. After selling his father's property, he married Lucy Bakewell of nearby Fatland Ford Plantation. They went to Kentucky in 1808 where the natural beauty and abundant wildlife of the frontier fascinated Audubon. He devoted more time to bird watching and drawing than to his commercial pursuits, which terminated in failure.

In 1820 he and his family, now including two sons, moved to Cincinnati, Ohio, where he worked for a short while as a taxidermist for the Western Museum, painted pastel portraits, and taught drawing. From Cincinnati, that same year, Audubon ventured down the Mississippi River to the lower Mississippi valley. He had decided to devote his life to portraying the wildlife of North America. It is at this point in Audubon's life that the preliminary drawings for the prints of the birds began, and therefore the time in his life where this book begins.

[1] Alice Ford, *John James Audubon*, (University of Oklahoma Press, Norman, Oklahoma, 1964) pp. 12-17. According to Alice Ford, authorities in Santo Domingo misspelled her name "Rabin," the spelling that appears on her burial certificate at Notre-Dame l'Assomption, Les Cayes.

[2] Stanley Clisby Arthur, *Audubon, an Intimate Life of The American Woodsman* (Harmanson, New Orleans, 1937), pp. 465-75; Francis Hobart Herrick, *Audubon the Naturalist*, 2 vols. (D. Appleton and Co., New York and London, 1917), vol. I, pp. 67-72 and p. 133.

PART I

The Birds

LOIS ELMER BANNON

CHAPTER I

The Preliminary Work

The Birds of America, by John James Audubon (1785-1851), exemplifies man's ability to accomplish an almost impossible task through sacrifice and persistence. Audubon set out to paint and publish an example of every bird on the North American continent, an endeavor that required tedious and time-consuming preliminary work in research, art, and promotion, and he persevered until he was satisfied. He traveled extensively throughout the United States and made one trip to Labrador. In addition, specimens of birds were sent to him from western North America. Four times he sailed to England to contract for and supervise engravings. He had a formidable assistant in his wife, Lucy Bakewell Audubon, who had become his bride in 1808. As his two sons, Victor Gifford and John Woodhouse, grew to manhood, they too became artists and joined his cause, along with other artists and naturalists.

From his childhood Audubon had been studying and drawing birds, a hobby that interfered first with his early education and later with his vocation as a merchant. At the age of thirty-five, bankrupt and disillusioned by what he called "the dull world of commerce," Audubon set out on his first trip for the specific reason of drawing birds for a folio collection that he hoped would in some way bring

financial rewards. He traveled down the Ohio and Mississippi rivers from Cincinnati to New Orleans, an area profuse
with local and migratory birds and known to ornithologists
today as the Mississippi flyway. In New Orleans in 1820, he
discussed the possibilities of an engraved folio with a friend.
His life from that time on was completely absorbed with
being an artist and naturalist. The last drawings for the elephant folio engravings were not completed until 1837.

Audubon's goal was to make life-size drawings for engravings of all the North American birds. He was the first
artist-naturalist to illustrate American birds, life-size, in natural poses; the backgrounds, or habitats, are more natural
looking than those of his predecessors. He painted his freshly
killed specimens before their colors faded and eventually
learned to wire his models in a lifelike manner. His first
drawings were in pencil and charcoal, but as he experi-
mented and learned he began to use pastels, oil, lacquer,
and even egg white. Mixed media, therefore, would aptly
describe his works. His goals and techniques were expressed
in his own words in 1838:

> The first collection of drawings I made were from Europe-
> an specimens, procured by my father or myself . . . . They
> were all represented strictly ornithologically which means nei-
> ther, more nor less than in stiff, unmeaning profiles, such as
> are found in most works published to the present day. My next
> set was begun in America, and there, without my honored
> mentor, I betook myself to the drawing of specimens hung by
> a string tied to one foot, having a desire to show every portion,
> as the wings lay loosely spread, as well as the tail. In this man-
> ner I made some pretty fair signs for poulterers.
>
> One day, while watching the habits of a pair of Pewees at
> Mill Grove, I looked so intently at their graceful attitudes that
> a thought struck my mind like a flash of light, that nothing,
> after all, could ever answer my enthusiastic desires to represent
> nature, except to copy her in her own way, alive and moving!
> Then I began again. On I went, forming, literally, hundreds of
> outlines of my favorites, the Pewees; how good or bad I cannot
> tell, but I fancied I had mounted a step on the high pinnacle
> before me. I continued for months together, simply outlining

birds as I observed them, either alighted or on the wing, but could finish none of my sketches. I procured many individuals of different species, and laying them on the table or on the ground, tried to place them in such attitudes as I had sketched. But, alas! they were *dead*, to all intents and purposes, and neither wing, leg, nor tail could I place according to my wishes. A second thought came to my assistance; by means of threads I raised or lowered a head, wing, or tail, and by fastening the threads securely, I had something like life before me; yet much was wanting. When I saw the living birds, I felt the blood rush to my temples, and almost in despair spent about a month without drawing, but in deep thought, and daily in the company of the feathered inhabitants of dear Mill Grove.

I had drawn from the "manikin" whilst under David,[1] and had obtained tolerable figures of our species through this means, so I cogitated how far a manikin of a bird would answer. I labored with wood, cork, and wires, and formed a grotesque figure, which I cannot describe in any other words than by saying that when set up it was a tolerable-looking Dodo. A friend roused my ire by laughing at it immoderately, and assuring me that if I wished to represent a tame gander it might do. I gave it a kick, broke it to atoms, walked off, and thought again.

Young as I was, my impatience to obtain my desire filled my brains with many plans. I not infrequently dreamed that I had made a new discovery; and long before day, one morning, I leaped out of bed fully persuaded that I had obtained my object. I ordered a horse to be saddled, mounted, and went off at a gallop towards the little village of Norristown, distant about five miles. When I arrived there not a door was open, for it was not yet daylight. Therefore, I went to the river, took a bath, and, returning to town, entered the first opened shop, inquired for wire of different sizes, bought some, leaped on my steed, and was soon again at Mill Grove. The wife of my tenant, I really believe, thought that I was mad, as, on offering me breakfast, I told her I only wanted my gun. I was off to the creek, and shot the first Kingfisher I met. I picked the bird up, carried it home by the bill, sent for the miller, and bade him bring me a piece of board of soft wood. When he returned he found me filing sharp points to some pieces of wire, and I proceeded to show him what I meant to do. I pierced the body of the fishingbird, and fixed it on the board; another wire passed above his upper mandible held the head in a pretty fair attitude, smaller ones fixed the feet according to my notions, and even common pins came to my assistance. The last wire proved a

delightful elevator to the bird's tail, and at last—there stood
before me the *real* Kingfisher.

. . . .

To me to study Nature was to ramble through her domains
late and early, and if I observed all as I should, that the memory
of what I saw would at least be of service to me.

. . . .

As I wandered, mostly bent on the study of birds, and with
a wish to represent all those found in our woods, to the best of
my powers, I gradually became acquainted with their forms and
habits, and the use of my wires was improved by constant practice. Whenever I produced a better representation of any species the preceding one was destroyed, and after a time I laid
down what I was pleased to call a constitution of my manner
of drawing birds, formed upon natural principles.

. . . .

The better I understood my subjects, the better I became
able to represent them in what I hoped were natural positions.
The bird once fixed with wires on squares, I studied as a lay figure before me, its nature, previously known to me as far as habits went, and its general form having been frequently observed.
Now I could examine more thoroughly the bill, nostrils, eyes,
legs, and claws, as well as the structure of the wings and tail;
the very tongue was of importance to me, and I thought the
more I understood all these particulars, the better representa-
tions I made of the originals.

My drawings at first were made altogether in watercolors,
but they wanted softness and a great deal of finish. For a long
time I was much dispirited at this, particularly when vainly en-
deavoring to imitate birds of soft and downy plumage, such as
that of most owls, Pigeons, Hawks, and Herons. How this could
be remedied required a new train of thought, or some so-called
accident, and the latter came to my aid.

One day, after having finished a miniature portrait of the
one dearest to me in all the world, a portion of the face was in-
jured by a drop of water, which dried where it fell; and although
I labored a great deal to repair the damage, the blur still remained. Recollecting that, when a pupil of David,[1] I had drawn

heads and figures in different colored chalks, I resorted to a piece of that material of the tint required for the part, applied the pigment, nubbed the place with a cork stump, and at once produced the desired effect.

My drawings of Owls and other birds of similar plumage were much improved by such applications; indeed, after a few years of patience, some of my attempts began almost to please me, and I have continued the same style ever since, and that now is for more than thirty years.[2]

At one time over a hundred of the drawings for the engravings were chewed up by rats that had penetrated the trunk where they were stored. Audubon did the drawings over again, and decided that they were better than the ones that had been destroyed. Most of Audubon's original studies for the engravings can be seen in New York City at the New-York Historical Society. This institution purchased 430 of them and other Audubon drawings from Mrs. Audubon in 1863. Since then other Audubon studies have been given to the Society. The engraved plates CCXCIII and CCCXCV were made from study plate 186, and the engraved plates CCCXCIX and CCCCXIV from study plate 327. The studies for plates LXXXIV and CLV are missing.

Some of these works are finished paintings, some are drawings, and some are drawing or painting sketches which the engraver finished. They were executed with the idea of their being used for engravings and not necessarily as finished paintings. The American Heritage Publishing Company has published an excellent book containing color reproductions of the original studies in the New York Historical Society collection.[3]

Audubon worked constantly to improve his drawing and painting techniques and studied under artists such as John Stein and Thomas Sully whenever he found the time. He was perfectly capable of drawing all of the elements in his studies himself, as is demonstrated in the painting, entirely by him, of the *Pinnated Grouse* or *Greater Prairie Chicken* (Havell CLXXXVI) (Illus. 1). However, he realized that if he were to complete the monumental task of finding, studying, and drawing all of the North American birds and seeing that the drawings of the birds were set in the proper backgrounds, he would need the assistance of other artists for the botanical elements and the landscapes.

Joseph Mason, his first assistant, had been a pupil of Audubon in Cincinnati and had shown promise of becoming an excellent botanical artist. When he was only thirteen years old, he accompanied the naturalist on the 1820 trip down the Mississippi River. Together they studied the plants which Mason, with his teacher's guidance, would draw for the habitats. Audubon and his young apprentice worked in the lower Mississippi valley for almost two years. The *Yellow Throated Verio* is an example of the fine work that resulted from this partnership (Illus. 2).

In 1828-29 when Audubon was working in the northeastern area of the United States, a landscape artist, George

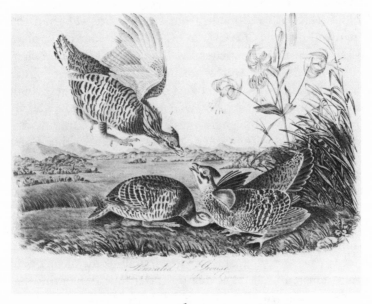

1.
Prairie Chicken or Pinnated Grouse
(Havell CLXXVI)

Yellow-throated Vireo or Greenlet.

2.
Yellow Throated Verio

Lehman, assisted him. Later he accompanied Audubon on his trips to the southeast coast and to Florida in 1831-32. The naturalistic landscapes of humid swamps and marshes, tropical river banks, and nineteenth-century towns are the work of Lehman. Well executed, they depict the proper environment for the birds without upstaging them (Illus. 3).

On a trip down the southeast coast in 1831, Audubon met in Charleston the woman who would be a loyal assistant for the rest of his life. She was Maria Martin, the sister-in-law of John Bachman, a Lutheran minister and an avid naturalist.[4] Bachman became Audubon's lifelong friend, opening his home to him and his family and assistants to live and work in whenever they were in the area, and eventually becoming the collaborator with Audubon on *The Viviparous Quadrupeds of North America*. Maria lived with the Bachmans. Besides helping her sister with a large family and a constant flow of guests, she drew illustrations

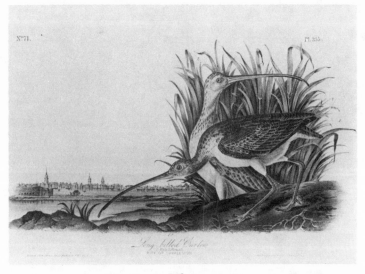

3.
Long Billed Curlew with Charleston in background
(Havell CCXI)

4.
Forked Tail Flycatcher
(Havell CLXVIII)

for Bachman's scientific papers. She also studied the flowers that grew in the prolific and well-tended garden that was both green and colorful with such plants as camellias, pomegranate and magnolia trees, vines of orange trumpet and wisteria, and annuals of all hues.

When Audubon first stayed at the Bachmans', he recognized Miss Martin's talents as a painter of flowers, butterflies, and insects. He encouraged her to spend more time at her art work and supplied her with art materials. Before his first long sojourn in Charleston was over, he was using her drawings for the backgrounds of the birds.

Usually Audubon first drew the bird. Then Maria would do the background foliage and branch on which Audubon would place his bird. The result was a well-composed, beautiful painting (Illus. 4). Later, when he was working elsewhere, she sent him drawings as he requested them.[5] Scholars who have studied her work have attributed the drawings of about twenty plants to her.[6]

The greatest assistance Audubon received came from his family and from his engraver, Robert Havell, Jr. By the time Audubon's son John was twenty-one, he was assisting his father in much of his art and research work. In a letter to Havell, Audubon defied Havell to tell his work from his younger son's. The American bittern in its habitat was completely drawn by John.[7] Victor painted several of the backgrounds in oil. He often stayed in England to supervise the engravings, sell subscriptions, and act as business manager. Havell saw the project through to its completion. He added to, deleted from, or changed compositions in 134 of the 435 drawings sent to him to be engraved.

Audubon credited his wife Lucy with the original study of the swamp sparrow, but it is suspected that Audubon did much of the work on this drawing.[8] Mrs. Audubon did indeed assist, but her greatest contributions to her husband's work were financial and literary. She worked as a tutor to support the family, leaving Audubon free to make field trips and seek engravers. From her salary she saved enough money to finance her husband's first trip to England. Later she collaborated with Audubon and William Macgillivray on the text which was published to accompany the prints of *The Birds of America*. Lucy was well aware of John Audubon's genius. Although her friends scoffed at her bird-chasing husband, she remained loyal to him and to his cause. Her devotion was rewarded by Audubon's love throughout his life, and she shared his fame when he was received by statesmen and presidents of the United States and by famous naturalists in England.

Most of the hunting and field studies were done by Audubon himself, but here also the right assistance was invaluable. Specimens had to be properly skinned and stored for collections and further scientific identification, a time-consuming chore because hundreds of birds were needed. John often helped his father with this phase of the work, especially on the New England and Labrador excursions. Henry Ward, a young English taxidermist, assisted Audubon in 1831 and went with him on the first trip to Charleston and Florida. When Audubon returned from the Florida expeditions, Charles Pickering, then curator of the Philadelphia Academy, identified the specimens and added further ornithological information. Dr. Richard Harlan of Pennsylvania, a physician and zoologist, exchanged information and specimens with Audubon and befriended him when he was unpopular with the Philadelphia naturalist clique. Except for Bachman, the American naturalist who gave Audubon the most assistance morally, financially, and scientifically was Edward Harris of Moorestown, New Jersey. Harris stored and shipped skins when directed, acquired subscribers, accompanied Audubon on the Gulf of Mexico trip in 1837, and at times aided him financially. Harris was instrumental in acquiring for Audubon from the Philadelphia Academy the skins from western North America that had been brought back by John Kirk Townsend and Thomas

Nuttall from their trip to the Rocky Mountains, an expedition Audubon had hoped to make but never did. Nuttall personally gave Audubon a few specimens.

As Audubon's fame spread, men who had at one time refused to help him came to his assistance. William Cooper of the New York Lyceum of Natural History had been uncooperative until Audubon returned to America from England as a renowned naturalist in 1836. Titian Peale, who had originally refused the use of his ornithological collection, later gave Audubon some fine specimens.[9]

In the third decade of the nineteenth century Audubon had no professional agent or advertising agency to aid him in selling subscriptions to the engravings of *The Birds of America*. Encouraged by new-found friends in England, such as the Rathbones of Liverpool and the famous British zoologist, Thomas Traill, Audubon exhibited his portfolio at public showings and wrote a text to accompany the prints. For promotional purposes he hired John Kidd, an English artist, to copy many of his drawings in oil. Audubon also prepared a prospectus and showed his collection publicly and privately in England, France, and America. Victor took charge of European sales and promotion when his father was in America. Nicholas Berthoud, Audubon's brother-in-law, eventually became the agent for the American market. The articles that Audubon was writing for professional zoological journals probably helped in securing subscriptions. Even some of his controversial pieces resulted in drawing attention to the self-made American naturalist.

From 1820 until 1837 Audubon was collecting specimens, making drawings, supervising engravers, selling subscriptions, writing a text, and writing for scientific journals. Through his own work and perseverance, and with the help of family, friends, and employed assistants he laid the groundwork for his famous bird engravings.[10]

1. Jacques Louis David (1748-1825). Whether or not Audubon studied with David remains controversial.

2. Maria R. Audubon, ed., *Audubon and His Journals*, (New York: Charles Scribner and Sons, 1899), 2:522-27.

3. John James Audubon, *The Original Water-color Paintings for The Birds of America*, (New York: American Heritage Publishing Co., 1966).

4. Audubon's sons married two of Bachman's daughters. After her sister died, Maria Martin married Bachman.

5. Buckner Hollingsworth, *Her Garden Was Her Delight*, (New York: Macmillan Co., 1962); W. O. Freeland, *A Survey Exhibition in Memory of Maria Martin*, (Columbia, S. C.: Columbia Museum of Art, 1964); Interview of Lois Bannon with Annie Roulhac Coffin, great-granddaughter of John Bachman, Nov. 8, 1970.

6. Audubon, *Original Water-color Paintings for The Birds of America*, 1:xxxi.

7. John also assisted greatly for the octavo edition and did at least half of the drawings for *The Quadrupeds*.

8. Audubon, *Original Water-color Paintings*, plate 331; See Chapter IX for table showing which assistant worked on each drawing.

9. Audubon had not acknowledged a hawk that Cooper had discovered and had named "Cooper's hawk." Audubon named the same hawk "Stanley's hawk," which, no doubt, helped to alienate Cooper. Titian Peale, the artist, was illustrating a book for George Ord, an avowed enemy of Audubon's. Peale was probably influenced by Ord.

10. In addition to those cited, general sources for this chapter are: Francis Hobart Herrick, *Audubon The Naturalist*, 2 vols. (New York and London: D. Appleton and Co., 1917); Stanley Clisby Arthur, *Audubon: An Intimate Life of The American Woodsman*, (New Orleans: Harmanson, 1937); Alice Ford, *John James Audubon*, (Norman: University of Oklahoma Press, 1964).

CHAPTER II

The Elephant Folio Engravings of The Birds of America (1824–38)

Engravers	William H. Lizars, Robert Havell, Jr.
Media	Watercolored engraving and aquatint
Size of paper	Elephant folio (same as double imperial type folio) size (29½ x 39½ inches untrimmed)
Type of paper	Two types of Whatman paper, one watermarked "J. Whatman/ Turkey Mill" and one water-marked "J. Whatman."
Number of plates	435
Number of complete folios published	Estimated between 161 and 175

Philadelphia was the hub of culture and of literary pub-lications in the United States in the early nineteenth century. It was there that Audubon took his work in 1824 when he had completed enough drawings to present for engravings; it was there also that he received a disappointing reception because of two influential men who were vitally interested in the success of the work of Alexander Wilson.[1]

One was George Ord, an established naturalist who had written Wilson's biography and had edited the eighth and written the ninth volume of Wilson's *Ornithology*. The other was Alexander Lawson, engraver of the bird illustrations for Wilson's book. Apparently both of these men looked upon Audubon as a threat and a rival. In Ord's opinion Audubon's drawings could not be studied scientifically because the birds were not in stiff profiles. Also, he felt that the botanical elements and landscapes detracted from the birds. Charles Bonaparte, [2] who was writing a general ornithological work, was enthusiastic about Audubon's drawings and introduced him to Lawson in the hope that he would want to engrave them, but Lawson pronounced them unsuitable for engraving. Another Philadelphia engraver, Gideon Fairman,[3] who was more appreciative of Audubon's drawings, advised him to go to England where he would be more likely to find an engraver with the abilities needed to properly reproduce his large, intricate work. From Philadelphia Audubon went to New York, where he was elected to the New York Lyceum of Natural History, but where he found neither interested publishers nor financial assistance for a trip abroad.

Two years later, in 1826, John James Audubon arrived in Liverpool to look for an English engraver. His trip was financed by money he and his wife had saved from teaching in Louisiana. While his wife had tutored in a private plantation home in West Feliciana Parish, he had taught art, dancing, French, and fencing in the same vicinity. This beautiful green country, where the huge, spreading live oak trees with their Spanish-moss laden branches provide ample perches for some of the most colorful birds in North America, was one of Audubon's favorite field study areas. Here he added drawings to his expanding folio while working and saving for his trip abroad.

In England, Audubon's reception was quite different from that in Philadelphia. The British were highly complimentary of Audubon's work. Richard Rathbone, a prominent citizen of Liverpool, and George Children, a naturalist and physicist who was secretary of the Royal Society of London, both acknowledged Audubon's letters of introduction with generous hospitality and introduced him to the British world of science and letters. Noted ornithologists such as Thomas Traill and William Swainson encouraged him to exhibit his work and publish a text. The popular portrait painter, Sr. Thomas Lawrence helped him sell his oil paintings. Sir William Jardine and Prideaux John Selby, British artist-ornithologists, took lessons from Audubon in delineating birds.

Almost everyone in Britain who saw Audubon's work was impressed with the dramatic, lifelike effect he had achieved in his bird paintings. The exception to this was Charles Waterton, an eccentric zoologist. He claimed that Audubon's drawings and writings were unscientific. When George Ord heard that Audubon had an adversary in England, he immediately wrote to Waterton. The two men became lifelong friends, devoting their time and energies to heckling Audubon, but they had little success in England, and eventually most Americans also ceased to take their diatribes seriously.[4]

Audubon's success among Britain's scientists is confirmed by the large number of professional organizations into which he was voted membership. They included the select Royal Society of Antiquarians and the Linnaean Society of London; this explains the letters "F.R.S." and "F.L.S." (Fellow of the Royal Society of London and Fellow of the Linnaean Society) after his name on the studies and engravings.

While exhibiting his folio in Edinburgh, Audubon met

William H. Lizars, who was the engraver for Selby's *British Birds*. The Scottish engraver was so impressed with Audubon's bird paintings that he was delighted with the opportunity to engrave them. "Mr. Audubon," he said, "the people here don't know who you are at all, but depend on it, they *shall* know."[5] Lizars contracted to do the first set of five plates, beginning with the *Turkey Cock*, which has become a symbol of John James Audubon. Well pleased with the results, Audubon hired him to complete the project, but while the second set of five plates was being engraved, the colorers went on strike. Lizars sent work to Audubon, who was in London, to find colorers there. As the strike wore on, it became evident that Lizars could not finish the folio and that Audubon would have to find another engraver. He was sent to an artist-engraver with an excellent reputation, Robert Havell, who protested that he was too old for such an undertaking. His son, Robert, Jr., also an excellent artist-engraver with exceptional abilities in etching and aquatint, agreed to contract for the job. Robert Havell, Sr., colored the plates and supervised a staff of colorers until 1830. Audubon thought the Havells' work surpassed that of Lizars. An added bonus was that it was less expensive.

Throughout the next eleven years either Audubon or his son Victor was in England personally supervising the engraving, printing, and coloring. The colorers, who at times numbered as many as fifty men and women, were sometimes reprimanded by Audubon when he thought their work was poorly done. Both Havells worked under direct verbal and written orders from Audubon.[6]

The first ten plates were engraved by Lizars in 1826 and 1827. The remainder of the plates were engraved in London by Robert Havell, Jr., who reworked several of Lizars's plates. Fifty of the first five plates were colored in Lizars's establishment, the rest in Havell's. The imprint legend on the lower left-hand side of the page reads, "Engraved by W. H. Lizars" or "Engraved by W. H. Lizars" and below,

"Retouched by R. Havell, Jr." on the first ten plates. Until 1830 the plate legends read "Engraved and colored by Robert Havell and son." Sometime after his father's death in 1832 Robert Havell, Jr., dropped the "Jr." Therefore some legends read, "Engraved and colored by Robert Havell, Jr." and some, "Engraved and colored by Robert Havell."

Audubon's drawings were transferred to large copper plates on which the delineations were engraved and aqua-

J WHATMAN
TURKEY MILL
1831

J WHATMAN
1837

tinted. Aquatinting is an etching technique. As most of the work is engraved, however, the finished prints are referred to as engravings. After being printed on Whatman hand-made drawing paper, the black and white engravings were watercolored by hand. The paper is elephant folio (or double folio) size, which in this case is 29½ x 39½ inches untrimmed. The name "elephant folio" is derived from the size of the paper, which is double the size of a folio sheet.

Two different types of Whatman paper were used. The first is watermarked "J. Whatman/Turkey Mill/1827 (to 1838)" and the second "J. Whatman/1827 (to 1838)." According to E. F. Hanaburgh, who studied the papers, the "Turkey Mill" paper is of lighter weight than the "J. Whatman." He notes that the "Turkey Mill" became draber with age and colors softened in tone, while the paper having only the "J. Whatman" watermark maintained a more brilliant appearance, if kept under proper conditions. Some collectors prefer the time-softened coloring; some like the brilliant appearance. The price is not affected by this difference. Hanaburgh has attempted, with no specific results, to date folios by the paper on which they were printed.[7]

Subscriptions were received throughout the eleven years of publication; therefore changes were made in some of the engraved copper plates which were printed over the eleven year period, a fact which explains the variations to be found not only in the subjects themselves but in legends, dates, and set numbers. For example, Howard Rice notes that in plate I, the famous *Wild Turkey*, there are at least three states of the engraved legend. In the first state the common name is given as *Great American Cock*, and the engraver's imprint is "Engraved by W. H. Lizars." In the second state the common name remains the same but "Retouched by R. Havell, Jr." is added below the original imprint. In the third state the common name is changed to *Wild Turkey*, while the double imprint remains.[8] Other examples of different states are noted by Waldemar Fries in a detailed study of the engraved elephant folio.[9] According to Taylor Clark there are no price differences in the various states of the same plate.

The entire set of engravings contains 435 plates depicting 1,065 life-size figures of birds. The scientific and common names of the birds were given on each plate. The legends contain the names of the author and engravers. The date of engraving does not appear on all of the plates.

The engravings were issued to subscribers in eighty-seven sets or parts, with five plates to a set. The sets are often referred to as "numbers." The plate number was sometimes engraved in Roman numerals and sometimes in Arabic numerals, whereas the set number is always in Arabic numerals. Each set of five plates originally sold for two guineas. The complete work sold in England for £182.14 and in the United States for $1,000. In 1973 a complete set was sold for $246,000. In 1977 a complete set sold for $396,000 at Christie's in New York. Also in 1977 the *Turkey Cock* in excellent condition sold for $18,000. Some of the warblers sold for $800. Plates that are badly faded, torn, flocked, folded, trimmed, or damaged in any manner are devalued as explained in Chapter XIII.

When requested by the subscribers, the plates were bound, usually in four volumes. The exact number of bound and unbound sets is not known. The complete sets engraved can be estimated between 161 and 175, the number of subscribers remaining on Audubon's list in 1838 and the number Victor Audubon estimated.[10] He received a total of 279 subscriptions, but many subscribers canceled or defaulted on payments after receiving part of the complete set. Therefore, there must have been many more impressions of the earlier plates printed. A number of uncolored plates were dispersed. Herrick notes that a complete set of uncolored plates sold at public auction in Philadelphia for three thousand dollars in 1907. He also reports that some individual uncolored engravings were given to friends as gifts from Audubon and his wife.[11] Waldemar H. Fries has taken a census of existing folios and has established the present location of 134 complete sets.[12]

The following chart shows the plates contained in each volume and the dates they were engraved.

Vol.	Sets of Five	Plates	Date
I	1-22	I-CX	1826-1830
II	23-44	CXI-CCXX	1831-1834
III	45-66	CCXXI-CCCXXX	1834-1835
IV	67-87	CCCXXI-CCCCXXXV	1835-1838

The dates of publication of the plates are: plates I to XXVII were published in 1826-27, plates XXVIII to L in 1828, plates LI to LXXV in 1829, plates LXXVI to C in 1830, plates CI to CXXV in 1831, plates CXXVI to CLV in 1832, plates CLVI to CLXXXV in 1833, plates CLXXXVI to CCXXXV in 1834, plates CCXXXVI to CCLXXXV in 1835, plates CCLXXXVI to CCCL in 1836, plates CCCLI to CCCC in 1837, and plates CCCCI to CCCCXXXV in 1838.[13]

The legend persists that all of the copper plates were destroyed by fire.[14] The truth is that some were damaged by fire during Audubon's lifetime. Some were saved by Charles A. Cowles from being melted down in a brass and copper company to which they had been sold about 1873.[15] There are some copper plates still in existence. They are owned by individuals and by public institutions. Some can be seen in the New-York Historical Society, the Metropolitan Museum of Fine Art, the American Museum of Natural History, the New York Botanic Gardens Museum, and the New York Zoological Society Museum, all in New York City; the Smithsonian Institution; Princeton University; Yale University; Johns Hopkins University; Wesleyan College; Groton School; Pratt Memorial Library in Cohasset, Massachusetts; Carnegie Library in Pittsburgh; Wadsworth Atheneum in Hartford, Connecticut; Pleasant Valley Bird Sanctuary in Lennox, Massachusetts; Rosedown Plantation House Museum in Saint Francisville, Louisiana;

and Audubon Shrine and Wildlife Sanctuary in Audubon, Pennsylvania.

There should be little difficulty in recognizing an original print from the engraved elephant folio edition of *The Birds of America*. The size of the untrimmed paper (29½ x 39½ inches) is the first clue; trimming is usually obvious. Often from half an inch to one inch is missing from the left margin where the print has been cut from the folio binding. A buyer or dealer should never hesitate to take a print out of a frame or from under a mat if he is not sure of the authenticity of the print.

The other original Audubon *Birds of America* prints which are almost the same size are the chromolithographed elephant folio edition discussed later in this book. It is not difficult to learn to distinguish a chromolithograph from an engraving. The printer's legend on the chromolithograph edition provides a further check; it reads "Chromolity by J. Bien, New York." The watermark is the next obvious clue. If the paper does not have a watermark as discussed above, it is not from the engraved elephant folio edition. It is difficult to see a watermark unless one holds a print so that strong light shines through the paper. This test may be necessary if the author and engraver legends have been cut off. The author's legend reads, "Drawn from Nature by John James Audubon, F. R. S., F. L. S. etc." on all Audubon prints, including most reproductions of the original Havell engravings. The printer's legend in the engraved elephant folio edition is discussed earlier in this chapter. Since Audubon did not copyright *The Birds of America*, many reproductions of the engravings do not have the printer's or publisher's name on the paper. Most, but not all, reproductions are printed on smaller paper than that used for the original Havell elephant folio engravings or Bien chromolithographs. One well-known reproduction is a multicolored offset copy of the entire Havell set of 435 prints. It is 28 x 39½ inches, almost the same size as the original elephant folio editions. The publisher's name is not printed on the paper, but the paper is watermarked clearly, "G. Schut & Zonen (R) Audubon." A complete set sells for around twelve thousand dollars, and is limited to 250 copies. It was printed in Amsterdam and is referred to as "The Amsterdam Edition." The Voyageur and Ariel Presses together have published a limited number of multicolored offset facsimiles of forty of the plates from the Havell edition. They are the same size as the original Havell engravings, but they are obviously offset prints and the paper on which they are printed does not have a watermark.

The engraved elephant folio edition of *The Birds of America* was published without text or table of contents.[16] John James Audubon and his wife, with William Macgillivray of the University of Edinburgh as scientific and general editor, wrote *Ornithological Biography, or An Account of the Habits of the Birds of the United States*. It was printed in five volumes and contained information about the birds in the engraved elephant folio edition in the order in which they appear in that edition.[17] Audubon also published in Edinburgh in 1839 *A Synopsis of the Birds of North America* in one volume.[18] This is an index and summary of *Ornithological Biography* and thus serves as an index for the large engraved edition of *The Birds of America*. *Ornithological Biography* was the basis of one of Audubon's next achievements, "The Birds in Miniature," or the octavo edition of *The Birds of America*.

1.   Alexander Wilson (1766-1813), an American who had emigrated from Scotland, was a weaver, poet, schoolteacher, and self-made ornithologist, wrote the third and one of the most important American ornithological works, illustrated by himself and Titian Peale. (The first two works about American birds were by Vieillot of France and Mark Catesby of England.) As an ornithologist-artist Wilson was the protege of William Bartram, Philadelphia botanist; Alexander Lawson, Wilson's engraver; and George Ord, ornithologist. Ord referred to Wilson as the "father of American ornithology," a title that correctly belongs to Vieillot.

2. Charles Lucien Jules Laurent Bonaparte (1803-57), prince of Canino and Musignano, was the nephew of Napoleon Bonaparte. He was staying in Philadelphia with his uncle and father-in-law, Joseph Bonaparte, the former king of Spain, when Audubon met him. Audubon illustrated the Boat-tailed Grackle for Bonaparte's book, *American Ornithology, or the Natural History of the birds of The United States, not given by Wilson.* Titian Peale did most of the bird illustrations for the book and Lawson was the engraver.

3. Fairman hired Audubon to draw a grouse which was engraved on a New Jersey banknote.

4. Often, to the detriment of Wilson, who was not alive to defend the writings Ord attributed to him, Ord and Waterton have intimated erroneously that Wilson and Audubon were rivals and forever feuding.

5. Herrick, *Audubon the Naturalist*, 2:358.

6. *See* Chapter I.

7. E. F. Hanaburgh, *Audubon's Birds of America*, (Buchanan, N.Y.: 1941), 3.

8. Howard C. Rice, Jr., "A Study of the Successive Stages and Techniques of Audubon's Elephant Folio Engravings," Princeton University Library *Chronicle*, 21, nos. 1-2 (1959-60): 42-49.

9. Waldemar H. Fries, *Double Elephant Folio, The Story of Audubon's Birds of America*, (Chicago: American Library Association, 1973), pp. 209-24, 421-39.

10. A final list of subscribers is in Herrick's *Audubon the Naturalist*, 2:380-85. Victor Audubon wrote that he thought there were about 175 sets printed, and that about 80 of these were in the U.S.A. This reference is from *Audubon and His Journal*, edited by Maria Audubon, 1:71. For more recent information about subscribers see Fries, *Double Elephant Folio*, pp. 141-71.

11. Herrick, *Audubon the Naturalist*, 2:190.

12. Fries, *Double Elephant Folio*, p. 196.

13. Stanley Clisby Arthur, *Audubon, An Intimate Life of The American Woodsman*, (New Orleans: Harmason, 1937), pp. 486-87.

14. Elenor Clark, "Audubon, The Last Days of Nature," *New York Review of Books*, 3, no. 10 (Dec. 31, 1964).

15. Herrick, *Audubon the Naturalist*, 2:307.

16. "The plates were published without any text, to avoid the necessity of furnishing copies to the public libraries in England agreeable to the laws of copyright." Joseph Sabin, *Sabin's Dictionary of America*, (New York: Sabin, 1868), 1:315, no. 2362.

17. John James Audubon, *Ornithological Biography*, 5 vols. (Edinburgh, 1831-39). Volume I also published in Philadelphia and Volume II in Boston.

18. John James Audubon, *A Synopsis of the Birds of North America*, (Edinburgh, 1839).

CHAPTER III

The Birds in Miniature
The Octavo Editions of
The Birds of America *(1840–71)*

Lithographer	John T. Bowen
Media	Hand-colored lithography
Size of paper	Royal octavo (in this case 6½ x 10 inches or 6½ x 10¾ inches, depending upon how it is bound)
Number of plates	500
Number of complete sets in first edition	Estimated at 1,200
Number of sets in later editions	Unknown

Audubon was still in England supervising the last engravings of the elephant folio edition of *The Birds of America* when he began planning for a smaller version to be published with a text similar to his *Ornithological Biography*. He would do more research and add new species. He would clarify the *Biography*, making it more like the *Synopsis*, and leave out the episodes or "delineations of American scenery and manners" which his friend Bachman referred to as "humbug." All this he did. The first royal octavo edition with texts of *The Birds of America* was published in New York and Philadelphia in 1840-44. It was a smashing success. Seven editions followed it; but the first truly looks like the miniatures of the famous engraved edition. Audubon referred to the royal octavo edition as the "petit edition" and "The Birds in Miniature."

The small editions contain hand-colored lithographs of sixty-five drawings by John James Audubon and camera-lucida copies by his son, John Woodhouse Audubon, of the elephant folio engravings. The size of the paper used for the prints and texts is royal octavo or one-eighth of a very large folio sheet. In this case the size is 6½ x 10 inches or 6½ x 10¾ inches, depending upon how the pages are bound. The prints were lithographed, printed, and colored by John T. Bowen and his assistants in Philadelphia under personal and written supervision from Audubon. At one time Bowen was so busy that he had to send some work to another lithographer, Endicott's of New York. At times Bowen had seventy people working on the prints. Often the initials of the artist who traced the drawing on the lithographic stone is placed in the print. Subscriptions for the first edition varied from at least 1,000 to almost 1,500. The total number of subscribers in Audubon's published lists was 1,198.[1]

When Audubon, at the age of forty-six years, returned to America for the last time in 1839, he and his family made New York their permanent home. It was not, however, the end of traveling for Audubon. He traveled frequently throughout the eastern part of the United States, and made one trip to Canada to promote the octavo edition and sell a few folios left from the elephant folio edition. He was also promoting another future project, *The Quadrupeds of North America*.[2] In 1843 Audubon made a trip up the Missouri River from Louisville on the Ohio River to

Fort Union, an American Fur Company trading post, on the Missouri River. The purpose of the expedition was to make field studies both for the octavo edition of *The Birds* and for *The Quadrupeds of North America*. He was accompanied by an old friend, Edward Harris, who financed part of the expedition and served as secretary. John G. Bell, a skilled naturalist-taxidermist from Spark Hill, New York, was hired as taxidermist, and Isaac Sprague, a carriage painter from Hingham, Massachusetts, was engaged as assistant. Sprague was also a naturalist-artist whose drawings of birds, plants, and landscapes had favorably impressed Audubon when he first saw them in 1840.[3] John and Victor Audubon remained in New York to work on the octavo *Birds* and *The Quadrupeds* drawings and take care of business matters.

Like the large edition of *The Birds*, the first royal octavo edition was issued in one hundred sets or "parts," or "numbers," of five plates to a set. The hand-colored lithographs with related texts were wrapped in blue paper covers on which the prospectus, agents, and lists of subscribers were printed. These wrapped sets of five lithographs each are rare and valuable. Subscribers who desired to bind their sets usually had them bound in seven volumes. Each set of five lithographic plates and texts originally sold for one dollar. A complete set originally sold for one hundred dollars. In the late 1970s a complete bound set in very good condition sold for over six thousand dollars.

The royal octavo edition is not exactly a small replica of the engraved elephant folio edition. More than one species is shown on some of the plates in the large edition, whereas only one species appears on each plate in the royal octavo edition and often the backgrounds are simplified (Illus.1). New species of birds and new plants appeared in this edition, and the birds are grouped in an orderly scientific manner instead of the unorganized manner of the elephant folio edition.

1.
Blue Grosbeak
(Havell CXXII)

Blue Grosbeak
(Octavo showing reduction in design)

Some of the new plants shown are probably the work of Maria Martin as well as of Sprague, for Miss Martin continued to send botanical drawings when requested. According to Sprague's Missouri expedition diary he drew birds and animals as well as plants during this trip, and these drawings were, no doubt, helpful to Audubon in some of his finished drawings.[4] Sprague's greatest assistance, however, was for the work on the *Quadrupeds*.

The prospectus of the royal octavo edition illustrates Audubon's ideas about its contents:

To those who have not seen any portion of Mr. Audubon's Original Drawings, it may be proper to state, that their superiority consists in the accuracy as to proportion and outline, and the variety and truth of the attitudes and positions of the figures, resulting from peculiar means discovered and employed by him, and his attentive examination of the objects portrayed during a long series of years. Mr. Audubon has not contented himself with single profile views, but in many instances has grouped his figures, so as to represent the originals in their natural avocations, and has placed them on branches of trees decorated with foliage, blossoms and fruits, or amidst plants of numerous species—some are seen pursuing their prey in the air, searching for food amongst the leaves and herbage, sitting on their nests, or feeding their young; whilst others, of a different nature, swim, wade, or glide in or over their allotted element. The insects, reptiles and fishes that form the food of some of the birds, have now and then been introduced in the drawings. In nearly every instance where a difference of plumage exists between the sexes, both male and female have been represented, and the extraordinary changes which some species undergo in their progress from youth to maturity, have been depicted.

The plants are all copied from nature, and as many are remarkable for their beauty, their usefulness, or their rarity, the Botanist cannot fail to look upon them with delight.

The particulars of the plan of the work can be reduced to the following heads:

1. The size of the work is royal octavo, the paper being of the finest quality.

2. The Plates representing the Birds are correctly reduced from the original drawings, and are coloured in the most careful manner.

3. The work will appear in numbers, on the first and fifteenth of every month.

4. Each number will consist of Five Plates, accompanied with full descriptions of the habits and localities of the birds, their anatomy and digestive organs (with occasionally wood cuts representing the latter) and will be furnished to subscribers for one dollar, payable on delivery.

5. The work will be published in accordance with a scientific arrangement of the genera and species, and will complete the Ornithology of our country, it is believed, in the most perfect manner.[5]

Prints from all of the royal octavo editions of *The Birds of America* can be identified by the size of the paper on which they are printed, 6½ x 10 inches (or 6½ x 10¾ inches); the media, black and white lithography that has been watercolored by hand; and legends. The lower left legend reads, "Drawn from Nature by J. J. Audubon F.R.S. F.L.S." The lower right legend reads, "Lithd. Printed & Cold. by J. T. Bowen Phila" or "Endicott, New York." Other small prints that approximate this royal octavo size are usually reproductions of the large Havell edition and often have legends of that edition on the reproductions.[6] The exception is a book published by Volair Limited in 1977 containing forty of the bird prints and text from the first royal octavo edition.[7] It is an exact size reproduction. The prints are offset four-color lithographs. The legends are also reproduced and the paper is a facsimile of the paper used for the original first edition. When removed from the bound book the prints could be mistaken for the original hand-colored lithographs printed from lithographic stones. By carefully examining the prints one can discern that they are offset color prints. The variation in color of a hand-colored print is impossible to reproduce in offset four color print. If necessary a magnifying glass should be used because the screening effect of an offset print can be seen easily under magnification. Volair Limited is planning to reproduce the entire octavo edition of *The Birds* and *The Quadrupeds*. An engraving of Audubon's Turkey Hen which was executed by Lizars for *The Naturalist's Library* is smaller than the royal octavo lithographs. Nevertheless, this engraving is sometimes confused with the royal octavo lithograph of the *Turkey Hen*.[8]

In 1978 the individual royal octavo lithographic prints in good condition sold for fifty dollars, except for the *Turkey Cock*. A print of this plate in pristine condition sold for one hundred dollars. Prints that are excessively trimmed, or damaged in any way are devalued. Often up to one-half inch has been improperly cut from the binding.

The first edition is the most valuable. Most of the individual prints from this edition are identified by the absence of a tinted lithographic wash in the background which is present in all later editions (Illus 2). Some plates, however, cannot be identified by this method. For example the background of plate number 374, *The American Egret*, is entirely colored in the first edition and cannot be distinguished from the same plate in later editions. The lithographs in all of the later editions are identical and of the same value. They can be identified by edition when seen in a bound book or when the title page or a copy of the title page of the book from which the individual print has been taken is available. The following information about each edition and the publishers' names and dates which appear on the title pages should be helpful in identifying editions.

The first edition was published in 1840-44 by John James Audubon in New York and by J. B. Chevalier in Philadelphia. Most subscribers bound their complete one hundred sets of five lithographs and text to a set in seven volumes. The prints in the first edition do not have the lithographic wash tinted backgrounds found on the same

2.
Red Breasted Snipe
(First edition Octavo)

Red Breasted Snipe
(Later octavo edition)

plates in subsequent editions (Illus. 2). Publication data on
the first edition follows:

Vol.	Parts	Plates	Date
I	1-14	1-70	1840
II	15-28	71-140	1841
III	29-42	141-210	1841
IV	43-56	211-280	1842
V	57-70	281-350	1842
VI	71-84	351-420	1843
VII	85-100	421-500	1844

The second edition was published in New York by Victor G. Audubon in 1856. It is like the first except that the
prints have tinted lithographic-wash background, and volume I has a steel engraving of John James Audubon by
H. B. Hall after a portrait by Henry Inman. This edition
was issued in seven bound volumes.

The third edition was published in New York by Victor
G. Audubon in 1859. It was issued from the publishing
house of Roe Lockwood and Son in New York. It is identical with the second edition except that the imprint on
the reverse of the title page reads, "Entered, etc., 1839,"
and "R. Craighead, Printer, Stereotyper, & Electrotyper,
Caxton Building, 81, 83, & 85 Center Street." It was bound
in seven volumes.

The fourth edition was published in 1860 by V. G.
Audubon and issued by Roe Lockwood and Son. It was
bound in seven volumes.

The fifth edition was published in 1861 by J. W. Audubon and issued by Roe Lockwood and Son in New York.
It was bound in seven volumes.

The sixth edition is entitled *The Birds of America, a
Popular and Scientific Description of The Birds of The
United States and Their Territories*, New York, 1863. It
is said to be in seven volumes. This mysterious edition has

never been seen by the author or any of Audubon's biographers. It was recorded by Herrick from Dr. Elliott Coues's information.

The seventh edition was issued by J. W. Audubon in New York in 1865. It was bound in eight volumes.

The eighth edition was published by George R. Lockwood, New York. There is no date in any of the volumes. According to Herrick it was published in 1871. Volume I contains a short, erroneous biography of Audubon by George R. Lockwood. It was bound in eight volumes.[9]

Complete octavo editions of *The Birds of America* can be found in some private collections. Many public and university libraries have a complete set. Libraries that do not own sets have information about where the nearest set can be seen.

A re-publication of the first edition was printed in 1967 by Dover Publications. It is octavo size, 5½ by 8½ inches, and is smaller than the royal octavo size. The prints of the birds are black and white offset prints, not lithographs. It is bound in paper in seven volumes. There is an introduction in volume I by Dean Amadon. The index in volume VII has been brought up to date in reference to scientific and common bird names.

Audubon was justly proud of the royal octavo edition, as he was of the engraved elephant folio edition. It is appreciated in the late twentieth century as much as or more than it was in 1840-44 when the first edition was printed.

1.   Herrick, *Audubon the Naturalist*, 2:217-218. Subscribers are listed at the back of volume I of first royal octavo edition of *The Birds of America*.
2.   See Part II.
3.   Unpublished biography of Isaac Sprague by his grandson, Isaac Sprague, Jr., Museum of Fine Arts, Boston, Mass.
4.   Isaac Sprague, unpublished diary in Boston Athenaeum.
5.   Herrick, *Audubon the Naturalist*, 2:214
6.   See Chapter II for Havell edition legends.
7.   Audubon, John James, *Selected Birds of America*, (Kent, Ohio: Volair Limited Co., 1977).

8.   Sir William Jardine, *The Naturalist's Library,* (Edinburgh: W. H. Lizars, 1843), 3: plate 2.

9.   Herrick, *Audubon, the Naturalist*, 2:404-408. Arthur, *Audubon, The National Union Catalog pre-1956 imprints*, p. 598. The above references were used to compile royal octavo editions of *The Birds of America* that contain the lithographic illustrations. The books printed with text only are not included.

CHAPTER IV

The Reissue of the Elephant Folio of The Birds of America (1860)

(The Bien Edition)

Lithographer	Julius Bien (1826-1909)
Media	Chromolithography
Paper	Elephant folio (in this case 27 x 40 inches), no watermarks
Number of plates	106
Number of complete sets	Estimated at between 50 and 100

John James Audubon died in 1851 at his home, Minnie's Land, on the Hudson River near New York City. At that time his younger son, John Woodhouse Audubon, was deeply engrossed in the drawings for *The Quadrupeds of North America*. When he finished that project, John began a new endeavor that possibly he and his father had discussed, a reissue of the elephant folio edition of *The Birds of America*. Chromolithography was becoming a popular medium in Europe, and John chose this method to reproduce his father's work. The drawings on the copper plates were transferred to lithographic stone and colored in the stone. This process required a stone plate for each primary color.

Julius Bien, the lithographer, had immigrated to the United States from Germany. He was also a cartographer and portrait painter. The maps he lithographed for the United States government earned him the reputation of being the finest American cartographer of the nineteenth century.[1] His work on the reissued elephant folio of *The Birds of America* is a milestone in American lithography. The plates were the first large chromolithographs made in this country and are examples of good quality nineteenth-century chromolithography. Roe Lockwood and Son of New York published the work. The plates are dated 1858, 1859, or 1860. The first and only volume was published in 1860.

Bien and J. W. Audubon attempted to renumber the plates to correspond with those in the royal octavo edition. Also they made changes in a few of the plates. Some of the backgrounds were changed (Illus. 1), and some of the single bird figures were grouped. The small birds, which appeared one to a page in the Havell edition, were placed two to a page in the Bien edition, some arranged side by side and some with one above the other (Illus. 2). In either case the legend in the Bien edition appeared at the bottom of the plate, with "Drawn from nature by J. J. Audubon F.R.S. F.L.S." in the lower left corner and "Chromolith by J. Bien, New York," followed by the date in the lower right corner. When some pages were subsequently cut in half in order that the birds might be framed separately, these legends were of course affected. If a single bird had been one of a pair placed *horizontally* on a page in the Bien edition, it retained only the part of the legend that appeared directly under it. On the other hand, when a page on which the birds were placed *vertically* was divided, the bird from the upper half of the page was left with no legend, the bird from the bottom half retaining both parts.

1.
Black Vulture
(Havell CVI)

Black Vulture
(Bien print showing difference in background)

The "right-hand" small birds from the horizontal arrangements, carrying only the Bien legend, and the "upper" small birds from the vertical arrangements, with no legend at all, can therefore sometimes be found at bargain prices because they are not recognized as Audubons by persons who are not familiar with the Bien edition placement.

The birds from the Bien edition can easily be distinguished from those of the Havell edition by the fact that they are chromolithographed, by the legend, and by the unwatermarked paper. These chromolithographs have always sold for less than the Havell engravings, but they are, nonetheless, collector's items because of their rarity and beauty. In a prospectus published in England, John Woodhouse Audubon priced the prints initially at £285. for a set of five prints, or one-half the price of the Havell sets.[2] In 1978 some of the small birds (two to a page) sold for

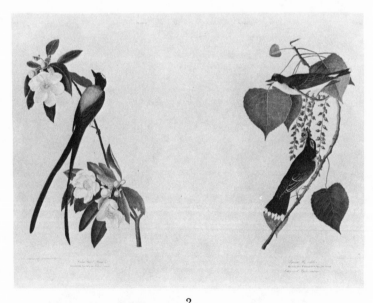

2.
Forked Tail Flycatcher and Tyrant Flycatcher
Two to a page. Bien edition.
Compare with Havell Forked Tail Flycatcher (Chapter 1, Illus. 4)

$200 to $600 a page and the larger birds for much more. (See chapter IX for individual print prices.) A complete folio sold for $30,000.

The term "original Audubons" as applied to the Bien prints has sometimes been questioned, but its validity seems fully justified even by the definition of an original print as authorized by the Print Council of America. In the mid-nineteenth century, when the Bien edition appeared, photo-reproductions were few in number and full color reproductions were nonexistent. There were no rules governing the use of the term "original print," and it was applied to the Bien edition with complete propriety. In the late twentieth century one might prefer to call the prints "original Bien and J. W. Audubon chromolithographs after J. J. Audubon," but a hundred years of usage supports the unqualified term "original." The value of the rare prints, whatever they may be designated, is the same.[3]

This edition is often described as ill-fated because it was never completed and was the financial ruin of John Woodhouse Audubon. The Civil War caused the work to cease and created financial problems. Octavo *Bird* and *Quadruped* subscriptions were still to be received and paid for by Southern subscribers and a large number of Southern subscribers for the Bien edition were eliminated. Only twenty-three subscribers can be accounted for. There were surplus plates, but how many has never been determined. Information about a Boston bookstore's buying large quantities of surplus plates, and John Woodhouse's statement in the prospectus that there would not be any more of the work published than the amount subscribed for, can probably be explained by inability to contact the Southern subscribers.[4]

The Civil War also plays the culprit in the fate of the stone plates: they had been stored in a warehouse in New Orleans and were destroyed when the warehouse was shelled.[5]

Yale and Harvard universities, the Brooklyn Museum of Art, the Flint, Michigan, and New York City public li-

braries are some of the institutions that own complete first
volumes of this edition. Single prints can be seen in Colo-
nial Williamsburg and the Audubon Memorial Museum in
Henderson, Kentucky. Many single prints and some first
volumes are in private collections. Waldemar Fries reported
he had located forty-nine copies of the one-volume Bien
edition.[6]

A text only of the royal octavo edition of *The Birds of
America* was issued by J. W. Audubon as a letter press to
the chromolithograph elephant folio. It was published by
Roe Lockwood and Son in New York in 1861.[7]

The Bien edition and the later royal octavo editions
were the last of the original *Birds of America* to be published
by Audubon's sons. The famous prints have continued to
be reproduced, by photographic methods, up to the present
day and are sought by ornithologists, bird lovers, artists,
art collectors, and botanists. The world, and especially
America, realizes the enormous debt owed to Audubon
and his family, not only for the *Birds of America*, but also
for the *Quadrupeds of North America*, which will be discussed in Part II.

1.   George C. Groce and Davis P. Wallace, *The New York Historical Society's
     Dictionary of Artists in America*, (Yale University Press, New Haven;
     Oxford University Press, London, 1957).

2.   Herrick, *Audubon the Naturalist*, 2:389.

3.   In the mid-twentieth century when interest in engravings, etchings, litho-
     graphs, and other fine print techniques was renewed, and photore-
     productions were plentiful, the need for a precise definition of an
     "original" print became increasingly apparent. The Print Council of
     America recommended a definition in 1961 that is widely accepted
     and complies with the standards set up in 1960 by The International
     Association of Plastic Arts, Unesco House, Paris. The definition is:
     "An original print is a work of art, the general requirements of which
     are: 1. The artist alone has created the master image in or upon the
     plate, stone, wood block or other material for the purpose of creating
     the print. 2. The print is made from the said material, by the artist
     or pursuant to his directions. 3. The finished print is approved by the
     artist. These requirements define the original print of today and do
     not in all cases apply to prints made before 1930." *Prints? What is an
     Original Print* (Print Council of America, 527 Madison Ave., New
     York, N.Y., 1961, 1964).

4. Herrick, *Audubon the Naturalist*, 2:297, 390, 391.

5. Alice Ford, *John James Audubon* (Norman: University of Oklahoma Press, 1964), p. 447.

6. Waldemar Fries, *The Double Elephant Folio*, p. 356.

7. Herrick, *Audubon the Naturalist*, 2:407; Arthur, *Audubon*, p. 492.

PART II

The Animals

LOIS ELMER BANNON

CHAPTER V

Preliminary Work for the Viviparous Quadrupeds of North America

John James Audubon is best known for *The Birds of America*. He was, however, the instigator of, and collaborator in, another important nineteenth-century work in the field of natural history, *The Viviparous Quadrupeds of North America*.

The octavo edition of *The Birds of America* was just under way when in 1839 Audubon decided to publish a large folio of North American mammals similar to that of *The Birds*, with an accompanying text. When his loyal friend John Bachman heard about these plans, he wrote to Audubon, "I am glad you are about to do something with regard to the small edition of *Birds*. But are you not too fast in issuing your prospectus of *The Birds* and *Quadrupeds*. . . . The animals have never been carefully described, and you will find difficulties at every step. Books cannot aid you much. Long journeys will have to be undertaken. Several species remain to be added and their habits ascertained. The drawings you can easily make if you can procure the specimens. I wish I had you here, if only for two days. I think that I have studied the subject more than you have. You will be bothered with the Wolves and Foxes, to begin with. I have two new species of Bats and Shrews to add. The Western Deer are no joke, and the ever varying

Squirrels seem sent by satan himself, to puzzle the naturalists."[1]

Audubon recognized the truth of this: he had little knowledge of the animals as compared with the vast knowledge he had acquired of the birds. Moreover, he was aging rapidly, far beyond his actual age of fifty-four years. He therefore heeded Bachman's advice and requested his collaboration. Bachman, with no recompense other than the hope of contributing to an investment that would return to two of his daughters, now married to Audubon's sons, unselfishly consented to assist with the text provided it was well done. "Our work must be thorough," he wrote, "I would as soon stick my name to a forged bank note as to a mess of soupmaigre."[2]

Unfortunately, neither Audubon nor either of his Bachman daughters-in-law lived to see the study of quadrupeds completed. Bachman did; in fact, his contribution to this work was so major that one can assume it would never have been accomplished without him. The Reverend John Bachman's studies and contributions in the field of natural history were as important to him as his duties as a minister, and he was highly respected in both fields. In order to devote as much time as possible to the quadrupeds, he turned down the position of president of South Carolina University. Besides categorizing and researching animals and writing most of the text, he was the driving force behind the completion of *The Quadrupeds*. In 1846 he married Maria Martin, who continued to draw for Audubon and to assist her husband in his research.

In the introduction to the forthcoming book Bachman and Audubon would write, "The Geographical range which we have selected for our investigations is very extensive, comprising the British and Russian possessions and America, the whole of the United States and their territories, California, and that part of Mexico north of the tropic of Cancer." This enormous undertaking required assistance from many other naturalists and more traveling for Audubon and his younger son, John Woodhouse.[3]

In order to publicize the new project and sell subscriptions to *The Birds*, Audubon traveled through New England and part of Canada, where he also procured quadruped specimens and information. In July of 1842 he went to Washington, D.C., and unsuccessfully tried to convince the United States government that it should sponsor a research trip to the Rocky Mountains. Although the mission itself failed, the effort was not lost, because while in Washington he met Pierre Chouteau, head of the American Fur Company, who offered transportation as far as the Yellowstone River. Audubon also was able to obtain letters of safe passage from President John Tyler and Secretary of State Daniel Webster.[4]

The following spring he began the westward trek to the Yellowstone, accompanied by Bell, Harris, and Sprague.[5] They covered much of the territory that had been explored by Lewis and Clark thirty-seven years earlier. Audubon was delighted with his first trip so far west and relished the opportunity to hunt buffalo with the Indians, but the results were somewhat disappointing to Bachman.[6] In a letter to Audubon he wrote, "For the last four nights, I have been reading your journal. I am much interested, though I find less about the quadrupeds than I expected. . . . your descriptions of Buffalo hunts are first rate."[7]

John Woodhouse Audubon made a field trip to Texas. He also went to England, where he used as models some of the animals in the London Zoological Gardens. Some excursions were much closer to home: permission was granted to the Audubons by the mayor of New York to shoot rats at the Battery for their rodent collection. Some models were literally available at home. By the time the Audubons had begun work on the quadrupeds, they were living outside New York City at Minnie's Land, an estate which derived its name from Lucy Audubon's nick-

1.
American Elk
(Plate LXII)
by J. J. Audubon (background probably by Victor Audubon)

name. This was a large tract of land overlooking the Hudson River.[8] Here they kept deer, elk, and other animals which could be used as live models. In addition to these resources, both Bachman and Audubon used skins of animals from all over North America which were sent to them.[9]

When about half of his drawings of the quadrupeds were completed, Audubon had a stroke that left him paralyzed and partially blind. John Woodhouse, who had become his father's number one art assistant, painted all of the remaining animals and finished sketches that Audubon had started. When drawing from specimens, both father and son used the technique that Audubon had devised for the birds, that is, wiring the specimens in lifelike positions. Unlike his father, John painted more often in oil than in watercolor. Their styles, however, are so similar that it is difficult to tell the sons's work from the father's. Although some of John Woodhouse Audubon's works are attributed to him in the legends, many are not; Audubon scholars agree that it seems hopeless to attempt exact attributions to some of the first seventy-eight plates (Illus. 1). John Woodhouse, who seldom signed his work, painted most of the animals for the last seventy-two plates in the imperial folio edition and the five additional plates in the royal octavo editions. Victor, Audubon's elder son, painted most of the backgrounds for the plates, assisted with editing and research, and handled business matters.[10]

The present locations of all of these original quadruped studies are not known. Some are in private collections and some can be seen in collections open to the public, such as those of the New-York Historical Society, the American

Caribou or American Reindeer
(Plate CXXVI)
by J. W. Audubon

Museum of Natural History, and the Pierpont Morgan Library in New York City, the City Art Museum and Boatman's National Bank in Saint Louis, the Audubon Memorial Museum in Henderson, Kentucky, and the National Gallery in Washington, D. C.[11]

The drawings that had been begun in 1840 were completed in 1848. By this time Bachman's daughters had both died, and Audubon's sons had remarried. They continued their close friendship with Bachman, however, who now solely for the sake of science supervised the remaining work during Audubon's illness and after his death. He also wrote the major part of a descriptive text that was published separately in three volumes to accompany the folio edition of the quadrupeds. Bachman was assisted in writing the text by Victor Audubon, using notes that Audubon and his other son, John W., had made on their research field trips as well as research by other naturalists.[12] Audubon's last illness prohibited him from contributing as he wanted to, and in what he did contribute, much of his colorful language was edited by Bachman. In 1851 Audubon died, before the last two volumes of the text were completed.

It was not until 1852 that Bachman could write to his friend Edward Harris, "Rejoice with me, the book is finished. I did not expect to have lived to complete it. But Victor Audubon came on, and I made him hold the pen, while I dictated with specimens and books before me, and we went on rapidly; we worked hard and now we are at the end of our labors."[13]

1.   Herrick, *Audubon the Naturalist*, 2:208, 209.

2.   Ibid, p. 211.

3.   John James Audubon and The Rev. John Bachman, *The Viviparous Quadrupeds of North America*, 3 vols. (New York: J. J. Audubon and V. G. Audubon, 1846-54), 1:vi.

4.   During this visit to Washington, D.C., Webster offered Audubon a government position, which he declined in favor of his less secure but more interesting life as an artist and naturalist. Ford, *John James Audubon*, pp. 392-393.

5. *See* Chapter III for further information about these men.

6. Maria Audubon, ed., *Audubon's Journal*, 1:453-532. Also for a good summary of the trip, *see* Ford, *Audubon's Animals*, Chapter 6.

7. Herrick, *Audubon the Naturalist*, 2:271-272.

8. This is now Washington Heights, 155 St. to 158 St.

9. Some of the men who sent specimens and assisted in examining them were Edward Harris, naturalist and close friend of Bachman and Audubon, (he helped to finance the Missouri trip to the Yellowstone); John K. Townsend, naturalist who had a large collection of mammals from his trip to the Rockies and westward; Spencer F. Baird, who became secretary of the Smithsonian Institution and founder of the United States National Museum and Bureau of Fisheries; Sir George Simpson, who sent specimens of arctic mammals; Pierre Chouteau, head of American Fur Company of St. Louis, who assisted Audubon's expedition to the Yellowstone; and W. O. Ayres, naturalist from Long Island.

10. In general it is assumed that Audubon did most of the small animals in the first seventy-eight plates and that John did the large ones. Alice Ford, *Audubon's Animals: The Quadrupeds of North America* (New York: Studio Publications, 1951), p. 15; Arthur, *Audubon*, p. 458; *Imperial Collection of Audubon's Animals*, ed. by Victor H. Cahalane (Maplewood, New Jersey: Hammond Inc., 1967), p. xiii; *Audubon and His Journals*, p. 70.

11. For other collections, public and private, *see* Ford, *Audubon's Animals*, pp. 215, 216; Ford, *J. J. Audubon*, pp. 449, 450.

12. *See* footnote 9.

13. Herrick, *Audubon the Naturalist*, 2:291.

CHAPTER VI

The Viviparous Quadrupeds
of North America (1845–48)

by John James Audubon
and The Reverend John Bachman

Published by	J. J. Audubon, New York
Lithographer	John R. Bowen
Medium	hand-colored lithography
Size of paper	imperial folio (28 x 22 inches)
Number of plates	150
Number of complete sets	estimated at 303

This handsome folio of four-legged North American mammals represents the work of John J. Audubon, John Woodhouse Audubon, Victor Audubon, John Bachman, and John Bowen, although the only names on the title page are those of J. J. Audubon and Bachman. John Woodhouse is credited in the legends for most of the animals that were entirely his work, but J. J. Audubon is given credit for animals that he had begun but that were completed by his son. Over half the animals, in fact, were the work of John Woodhouse.[1]

Victor Audubon, the elder son, painted most of the backgrounds, but in line with the customary practice of the nineteenth century, the background painter received no credits in the legends, so his name does not appear at all within the folio. In addition to Victor's artistic contribution, he also took care of the business matters pertaining to the folio and oversaw much of the lithography.

John Bowen, the lithographer for the octavo editions of *The Birds of America*, did an excellent job of reproducing the Audubons' animal studies in black-and-white lithography. Under his and Victor's supervision his staff then adeptly watercolored each print to match the colors in the watercolor and oil paintings.

The plates were issued to subscribers in 30 parts of 5 plates each, making a total of 150 plates. The size of the plates is imperial folio, which in this case is 28 x 22 inches. They were usually bound in three volumes. Volume I (parts 1 to 10, plates 1 to 50) was published in 1845. Volume II (parts 11 to 20, plates 51 to 100) was published in 1846. Volume III (parts 21 to 30, plates 101 to 150) was published in 1848.[2] The animals are not grouped according to species. There were at least 303 complete sets printed. This number is determined by the number of subscribers listed in the text that was published to accompany the folio. It is possible that more folios were printed, but probably not more than 350 or 400.

The lithographs sold for $10 a part, or $300 for the complete set when they were published.[3] The individual prints sold for $195 to $850 in 1977. An entire set sold for $18,000 in 1971. In 1979 a complete set in excellent condition sold for $38,000.[4]

The plates from the imperial folio edition can be recognized by their size. There have never been any reproductions of these lithographs in the original size to the knowledge of the author. The medium of hand-colored lithography and the legends also identify this edition. The bottom left legend is "Drawn from Nature by J. J. Audubon,

F.R.S. F.L.S." or "Drawn from Nature by J. W. Audubon."
The bottom right legend is "Lith. Printed & Cold by J. T.
Bowen, Phila." Complete sets can be seen at the High Art
Museum in Atlanta, Georgia, and the Museum of Natural
History and the Pierpont Morgan Library in New York
City.[5]

A three-volume text, royal octavo size (7 x 10½ inches),
was published to accompany the imperial folio edition.[6]
Its third volume included, in addition to the text, six color
plates of nine animals that were not in the imperial folio.[7]
This text also was named *The Viviparous Quadrupeds of
North America*. It was written mainly by John Bachman,
assisted by Victor Audubon.

When the last volume of the lithographs was published
in 1848, John James Audubon was too ill to enjoy the sat-
isfaction of a goal achieved. He was living in his comfortable
home at Minnie's Land, where his sons were also living and
working to complete his last project. There in 1851 Audubon died. His sons and his friend, Bachman, completed the
project and subsequently produced octavo editions. Although *The Quadrupeds* has not achieved the popularity
of *The Birds*, it is significant to the student of American
natural history and the collector of prints.

1.   Maria Audubon, ed., *Audubon and His Journals*, 1:70; Ford, *Audubon's
       Animals*, p. 15.

2.   Arthur, *Audubon*, p. 493.

3.   Ibid.

4.   Price information from Taylor Clark.

5.   For small color photographs of a complete set, *see The Imperial Collec-
       tion of Audubon Animals*, edited by Victor H. Cahalane. See also
       Audubon's Animals, by Alice Ford, for black and white and color
       photographs of the lithographs.

6.   Volume I was published by J. J. Audubon and V. G. Audubon in New
       York, 1846, and by Wiley and Putnam in London, 1847. Volume II
       was published by V. G. Audubon, New York, 1851. Volume III was
       published by V. G. Audubon, New York, 1854.

7.   The *Mountain Brook Mink*, the *Jackall Fox*, the *Weasel-like Squirrel* and
       the *Large Louisiana Black Squirrel*, the *Col. Abert's Squirrel*, the
       California Gray Squirrel, the *Harris Marmot Squirrel*, the *California
       Meadow Mouse*, and the *Crab-eating Raccoon*, all by John Woodhouse
       Audubon.

CHAPTER VII

The Quadrupeds of North America, *Octavo Editions (1849–54)*

**by John James Audubon
and The Reverend John Bachman**

Published by	Victor G. Audubon
Lithographer	John R. Bowen (except for 17 plates by Nagel and Weingaertner)
Medium	hand-colored lithography
Size of paper	royal octavo (7 x 10½ inches)
Number of plates	155
Number of complete sets in first edition	estimated at 2,004
Number of complete sets in later edition	unknown

The imperial folio of *The Viviparous Quadrupeds of North America* was still in production when Bachman convinced Audubon's sons that an octavo edition should be published also. "Viviparous" was dropped from the title, and the plates of the imperial folio and its accompanying octavo text, with five of the additional plates, were produced in royal octavo size to match the small *Birds*. The first volume was published in 1849, when John James Audubon was too ill to realize what was being accomplished. John Woodhouse Audubon reduced all of the large plates by the camera lucida method, just as he had reduced those of *The Birds*. Victor Audubon once again worked on backgrounds, oversaw the lithographers, secured subscribers, and published the works.[1]

John Bowen lithographed, in black and white, all of the plates except for seventeen in volume I which were lithographed by Nagel and Weingaertner. The plates were hand-colored by colorers of the lithographic establishments. Artists who reproduced the animals on the stone signed their names in most of the plates. The legend reads as follows: lower left, "Drawn from Nature by J. J. Audubon F.R.S., F.L.S." or "Drawn from nature by J. W. Audubon;" lower right, "Lith Printed & cold by J. T. Bowen, Phil.," or "Printed by Nagel & Weingaertner, N.Y.;" in the center above the name of the animal, "On Stone by Wm. E. Hitchcock" or "Drawn on Stone by R. Trembly."[2] (Illus. 1)

With the exception of *Selected Quadrupeds of North America* published by Volair Limited any small reproductions of the Quadrupeds are from the Imperial folio of *The Viviparous Quadrupeds of North America.*[3] In 1977 Volair Limited published the above mentioned book containing thirty-seven animal prints and the accompanying text from the original first octavo edition of *The Quadrupeds of North America*. It is an exact size reproduction in offset four-color lithography. How to discern the difference between the offset prints and the original lithographs is discussed in Chapter III. Volair Limited is planning to reproduce the entire octavo edition of *The Quadrupeds*.

The first edition was published by V. G. Audubon in parts of five lithographs with accompanying text. Each part sold for one dollar. The edition was distributed to

1.
Rocky Mountain Neotemo
Octavo Quadruped by Bowen

Rocky Mountain Neotemo
Octavo Quadruped by Weingartner

subscribers either in parts or bound in three volumes. Volume I (parts 1 to 10) was published in 1849, volume II (parts 11 to 20) was published in 1851, and volume III (parts 21 to 31) was published in 1854. There were apparently slightly more than 2,000 complete sets of the first edition published, as the number of subscribers reported by Herrick is 2,004.[4]

The second edition, which is identical with the first, was published by V. G. Audubon in three volumes. Volume I was published in 1852 and volumes II and III in 1854.

The third edition was published by V. G. Audubon in three volumes in 1856-60.

The fourth edition was published by G. R. Lockwood in three volumes in 1870.[5]

A complete set sold for thirty-one dollars when the royal octavo *Quadrupeds* were published. In 1978 a complete set in excellent condition was worth two thousand five hundred dollars, and individual lithographs sold from twenty to fifty dollars.

In 1858 the United States secretary of state was authorized to buy one hundred copies of the royal octavo edition both of *The Birds of North America* and of *The Quadrupeds of North America*, at a total cost of sixteen thousand dollars to present to foreign governments in return for valuable works sent by them to the United States government.[6] The choice of these works for such a purpose is a tribute to John James Audubon and a recognition of his art and of his unique contribution to American natural history.

1. Herrick, *Audubon the Naturalist*, 2: 292,293; Ford, *Audubon's Animals*, p. 21.
2. In the royal octavo *Quadrupeds*, J. W. Audubon was credited with ten plates that had been attributed to J. J. Audubon in the imperial folio.
3. Audubon, John James and Bachman, The Rev. John, *Selected Quadrupeds of North America*, (Kent, Ohio: Volair Limited Co., 1977).
4. Arthur, *Audubon*, p. 494; Herrick, *Audubon the Naturalist*, 2:391, 406.
5. *The National Union Catalog Pre-1956 Imprints*, p. 601; Arthur, *Audubon*, pp. 493-94.
6. Herrick, *Audubon the Naturalist*, 2:294.

PART III

The Birds and the Animals

TAYLOR CLARK

CHAPTER VIII

An Evaluation of the Editions of The Birds and the Animals

Audubon Prints by Havell have been sought after since the days they were printed. Some subscribers defaulted after receiving a certain number of prints and many of these found their way to the walls of English and American homes as early as the 1830s. Surely they were novelties of the time to some people who had never seen a *Wild Turkey, Whooping Crane* or *Great White Heron*.

Audubon Prints have been sold for comparatively low prices as late as the 1940s when the engraved *Turkey Cock* brought $500 and the *Song Birds* fetched as low as $7.50 each. The supply of prints was relatively plentiful and the sets of books available most of the time.

Today, we find that demand for Audubon prints has long passed the supply available and prices have increased very rapidly. Complete sets of Audubon's works are now almost totally absorbed by museums and public institutions. This leaves the source of prints practically extinct in large numbers and hence makes those available that much more valuable. (Most any active art dealer will recommend Audubon prints as fine works of art and good investments also.) Some of the larger birds, in the Audubon prints, have already reached the $18,000 price level and prospects are unlimited as to future prices.

Of course, certain requirements are necessary for an Audubon print to be desirable. Ideally, the print should be full size, untrimmed, or approximately 26 x 39 inches. A variance of 2 inches either way is acceptable because binders trimmed them shortly after they were printed and binders did vary slightly in the size of the books. Another important feature to consider is whether the print is mounted or glued to another surface. This is highly undesirable since many glues are of a damaging formula that permanently stains the print.

Some mounting processes have been gentle to the print and therefore less of a problem and acceptable as far as collecting the print. Also, some mountings, such as the cloth type, can be removed from the print. This is advisable if the print can be removed with no damage.

One of the most common problems of the Audubon prints is stains. "Foxing" or browned areas of the prints are, unfortunately, fairly common. If the stains are such that they do not interfere with the beauty of the print, they too can be acceptable. This problem is more noticeable in the smaller bird prints where more white paper is exposed. In the large prints, such as the *Turkey*, many stains can be hidden by the designs and colors. There are ways to remove most stains but it is a time-consuming task that requires skill and knowledge and should not be attempted by amateurs. Use only qualified restorers on Audubon print restoration. Offset staining is another type stain found on Audubon prints. This stain is caused by dark colors, such as in the *Vultures, Hawks,* and *Ducks*. The stain penetrates the prints in front of the dark color usually. The stain can reach the print behind also, usually not as damaging.

Other type damages are tears in the prints and creases in the prints. Small tears on the edges of the prints are common and acceptable in a collector print. Obviously, long tears into the composition of a print are undesirable and usually unacceptable in a collector print. Tears can usually be repaired neatly with linen tape on the back of the print. Again, this tape needs to be the correct type and professional advice should be secured before using any tape. Creases are fairly permanent in most prints and it is most difficult to remove them from Audubon prints. The first and last prints in each book are usually the ones with the worst crease problem. It seems that over the years, as the books were handled and viewed, people were careless in closing the books and from time to time the first and last few prints would be creased. If the books were stored for a lengthy time, the crease became fairly permanent in the paper. The prints with these problems will usually be plate 1—*Turkey Cock;* plate 100—*White Bellied Swallow;* plate 101—*Raven;* plate 200—*Shore Lark;* plate 201—*Canada Goose;* plate 300—*Golden Plover;* plate 301—*Canvas Back Duck;* plate 400—*Arkansas Siskin;* plate 401—*Red Breasted Merganser;* and plate 435—*Columbia Water Ouzel.*

There was at least one complete book and probably a whole set of Audubon prints that were folded and then bound in books. Evidently someone wanted smaller books and naturally the folded prints presented smaller books in height. The folds in these prints are obvious and completely unremovable. The prints can be enjoyed but they must be classified as less desirable, and therefore less valuable, than the unfolded prints.

In looking at an Audubon print from the front, one will notice numbers on the top and writing on the bottom. The numbers usually are roman numerals on the right, which is the plate number, and arabic numerals on the left, which is the set number of a group of five sent to the subscribers. The roman plate numerals on the right are in sequence of 1 to 435. The plate numbers can be in arabic, especially early plates, and the plate numbers can also be on the left sometimes, and sometimes in the middle top of the page. The arabic numeral usually on the left designating the group or set number is the most confusing number. The Audubon plates were issued five at a time to the subscribers. The set of five prints had sequence. There would be one large bird, one middle size bird and three small birds in each group. Each of these five prints would have the same arabic numeral on the left side. For example, plate 1—*Turkey*, through plate 5—*Bonaparte Flycatcher*, will have number 1 on them. If you divide five into the four hundred thirty prints, you will see there are eighty-seven groups of five.

In the lower left hand corner will be "Drawn from nature by J. J. Audubon F.R.S. and F.L.S." The J. J. stands for John James. The F.R.S. stands for Royal Society of London. The F.L.S. stands for Fellow Linnaean Society. These societies were groups of interested scholars, scientists, and ornithologists that had a common interest in discoveries of new species of birds and their studies. Audubon was very proud of his election to these eminent groups.

In the lower right corner several combinations of names may appear. One may well be "Engraved by R. Havell, Jr. and Printed and Colored by R. Havell, Sr. London." A second may well be "Engraved, Printed & Colored by R. Havell London" and then usually a date following this, although the date is not necessary. The third way is "Engraved by W. H. Lizars, Edinburgh" with no reference to Havell. Another way is with the Lizars name as above and then in smaller print underneath and to the side, "Printed & Colored by R. Havell, Sr." or "Colored by R. Havell, Sen."

The lower center section will give the name of the bird in English with the description of male or female and young. There will also be a subtitle in Latin for the bird. Below this will be the English and Latin title for the plate. On some prints there will be a view of a particular city which will also be noted in the center bottom of the plate. Also on some plates will be the plant, flower or tree that is illustrated. This name will be in English and Latin.

Some of the plates were re-designed over the eleven years. Usually the name of the bird was in a rather fancy script in the early years, 1827-30, and then changed to a plainer design in the years 1834-38. This re-designing will naturally only be found in the earlier plates since later plates were used without much interruption in subscriptions and hence were never re-designed. Mr. Waldemar Fries in his book, *The Double Elephant Folio* lists the prints he has researched with their variations of legends, designs, and types of paper used.[1] These variations or states do not affect the price of the print.

There were two types of paper used on the Havell Audubon prints. The first was watermarked "J. Whatman" with a date ranging from 1827-38. This paper was more white in appearance than the other paper. The second paper used had "J. Whatman" in the watermark with the name *Turkey Mill* underneath and also the date *(see illustration).* This paper was more cream or eggshell than the other paper. The second paper was used only when the first paper became temporarily out of stock. Both papers were of the same quality, making either one acceptable to the collector.

J WHATMAN
TURKEY MILL
1831

J WHATMAN
1837

The reader will find each Audubon-Havell print and its price in the next chapter. There is a formula used in pricing the Audubons considering each print is in equal condition. Of course, prints of popular and famous birds like the *Turkey Cock, Mallard*, and others command the top prices. The *Turkey Cock* brings more money than the *Whooping Crane*, although they are the same size.

There are three basic sizes of the Audubon prints. The large ones where the engraving line usually does not show because the composition takes up most of the page, the middle size ones averaging about 17 x 24 inches and the small ones about 12½ x 19½ inches. These sizes are the engraved areas only. The small size prints with one or two birds and very little foliage are not as valuable as the prints with three or four birds and beautiful flowers in the composition. You might say each bird adds a certain amount of value to the print. The same is true of the middle size and larger prints. The beauty and amount of color in a print affects its value; the more color, usually the more desirable. Some of the most prized prints are the extinct birds for obvious reasons. Generally the birds more people see are the most popular and hence the higher priced prints. This group includes the yard birds and game birds. The last element in judging the price of a print is sheer composition and beauty.

The Bien edition of the Audubon prints, in double-elephant folio size, was done in 1859-60. Comparatively little is known about the Bien prints as far as number done and the fate of the plates. Probably relatively few books were completed. John Woodhouse Audubon intended to re-issue the complete 435 prints. The Civil War severed the subscribers in the South and the project fell into bankruptcy. Only 106 prints were completed showing 150 of the Audubon designs. Many of the small bird prints were done two on a page. Some of the designs were vertical and some horizontal. The Bien prints are chromolithographs, which means they were printed design and color on the paper at the same time. This process gives a slight blur to the edges of the design and the whole effect is less precise than the Havell prints. The backgrounds were changed on some of the Bien prints. Usually Bien added design and background where there was none on the same Havell prints. In the lower right corner will be "Chromolith by J. Bien, New York 1860 (or 1858 or 1859)." The Bien prints have different plate numbers and set numbers than the Havell prints.

A few Bien prints examined by the author appear to have been hand-colored to highlight certain areas of the composition, whereas most are not. This highlighting has not affected the price of the prints.

Only in recent years have the Bien prints become more important to collectors. They are rare, possibly more rare than the Havell edition prints. They are not as highly prized as Havell prints because the detail is not as fine. As such, the Bien prints are not as valuable as the Havell prints. They are important and excellent examples of some of America's first large lithograph works. In 1979 a complete set sold for $38,000.

Audubon did the birds in miniature or small size after completing the Havells in 1838. The prints are usually known as the "octavo Audubon prints" because of the size of the books that contained them. Octavo refers to the size of the print page, 6¾ x 10 3/8 inches. The first edition of these octavo bird prints done in 1840 do not have a colored background; the later editions do. These prints are hand-colored lithographs done by Bowen in Philadelphia. Because of the size, the composition had to be altered on many of the prints. That is, in most cases, birds were left out of some compositions where four or more birds existed on the Havell plate. Many of the octavo birds will therefore differ slightly in composition from their Havell counterpart. The octavo Audubons, especially the first edition, are very fine prints and are worthy additions to any collection. There were 500 prints in the octavo size or 65 more than in the Havell books. "48 of these are different and revised versions, and 17 are entirely new, the results of Audubon's last journeys." The 17 prints that are new species, drawn by Audubon in 1843 on the Missouri River expedition, become more important because they were not in the Havell edition. The prints are plates 484-500 in volume VII. They are:

Plate 484 — *Harris's Finch*
Plate 485 — *Bell's Vireo*
Plate 486 — *Sprague's Missouri Lark*
Plate 487 — *Smith's Lark Bunting*
Plate 488 — *Le Conte's Sharp Tailed Bunting*
Plate 489 — *Missouri Meadow Lark*
Plate 490 — *Yellow-bellied Flycatcher*
Plate 491 — *Least Flycatcher*
Plate 492 — *Brewer's Black Bird*
Plate 493 — *Shattuck's Bunting*
Plate 494 — *Missouri Red-moustached Woodpecker*
Plate 495 — *Nuttall's Whip-Poor-Will*
Plate 496 — *Texan Turtle Dove*
Plate 497 — *Western Shor Lark*
Plate 498 — *Common Scamp Duck*
Plate 499 — *Common Troupial*
Plate 500 — *Baird's Bunting*

A complete first edition octavo set of *The Birds of America* with the bindings and pages in excellent condition is valued at $6,500 today. A later edition in excellent condition is $4,500. The individual prints range from the *Turkey Cock* which is now worth $100 to the less popular birds which are worth $30 when in good condition.

The Audubon *Quadrupeds of North America* are still unknown to some people. Audubon's birds are household names, of course. *The Quadrupeds* prints were lithographed and then hand-colored by Bowen in Philadelphia. Audubon became ill and did not finish this work. His sons, John Woodhouse and Victor, finished *The Quadrupeds*. Most of the animals are well done, including some superlative prints such as most of the squirrels, the cats, rabbits, foxes, raccoon, and opossum. Other prints collectors find very desirable are the *House Mouse, Striped Skunk, Elk, Deers, Bisons*, and the *Collared Peccary*. In chapters five and six the attributions of the quadruped lithographs are explained. The attributed artist (J. J. or J. W. Audubon) does not affect the price which is given in the next chapter.

The Reverend John Bachman, Audubon's friend from Charleston, was the collaborator on *The Quadrupeds* and contributed greatly to the text and supervision of the work.

The Audubon animals in octavo were finished in 1856, five years after Audubon's death. The 155 prints comprising a set, five more than the large Animal books had, usually appear in three volumes. The size is 6¾ x 10 3/8 inches, the same as the octavo birds. The five plates executed in this size and not the larger size are:

Plate 151 — *Jackall Fox*

Plate 152 — *Weasel like Squirrel and Large Louisiana Black Squirrel*

Plate 153 — *Col. Abert's Squirrel and California Gray Squirrel*

Plate 154 — *Harris' Mormat Squirrel and California Meadow Mouse*

Plate 155 — *Crab-eating Raccoon*

A complete octavo edition of *The Quadrupeds of North America* with the binding and pages in excellent condition is priced $2,500 today. The individual prints range from $50 to $20 when in good condition.

Proper framing of Audubon prints is a very important item for the prints' preservation. In discussing the subject of proper framing, we are explaining the most desirable method of displaying a print for enjoyment and yet protecting the print in the best manner. Unfortunately, over the years, many Audubon prints have been improperly framed and the prints have suffered irreparable damage.

Many prints were trimmed to fit smaller frames or for condensing their size. Many prints were mounted to remove all waves or wrinkles in the paper. Many times the prints were put in frames and simple corrugated cardboard put on the back next to the print. Of course, now we know that corrugated cardboard, especially the olden type, was highly acidic with glue and eventually stained the print next to it. Evidence of this problem can be seen on some prints by the presence of stain lines showing the design of the cardboard. Also, gummed tape was used to seal the area between the cardboard and frame and this tape split and loosened frequently allowing moisture, bugs, and dust to find its way behind the print and also in front of the print, naturally causing damage to the print. In defense of the framing industry, great strides have been made toward proper protection of important prints. The average framer today is usually aware of proper protective methods, whereas twenty or forty years ago custom framing was a simple, unsophisticated sideline in most instances. The whole framing industry has made tremendous advances in the past ten years.

The proper method to frame Audubon prints or any fine print is to have only museum rag board touching the print (see illustration). Museum board is a rag content board that has no damaging acid content. A person having an Audubon print framed should question the framer and be assured that the framer uses and knows the proper method of protective framing. Proper protective framing can be as decorative as one wishes. The protective board is actually not seen.

1.   Waldemar H. Fries, *The Double Elephant Folio* (Chicago: American Library Association, 1973) pp. 209-224, 421-436; *See also* chapter II.

FRAMING WITHOUT A MAT

Plexiglass

Museum
Board
Fillet

Print

Museum Backing

Card Board Backing

Strong paper
glued to frame
and covers entire
back of picture

FRAMING WITH A MAT

Plexiglass

Mat

Museum
Board
Fillet

Print

Museum Backing

Card Board Backing

Paper as above

CHAPTER IX

Print by Print

The following tables are included in this handbook to enable the reader to know the price range of each print in the Havell and Bien editions of *The Birds of America* and the large edition of *The Viviparous Quadrupeds of North America*. The price is indicative of a print in excellent condition. The price could vary as much as fifty percent lower for a print in very bad condition.

The tables also include where the original bird study was painted and the artist assistant. Information about the place and the assistant artists is from Stanley Clisby Arthur's *Audubon: an Intimate Life of the American Woodsman* and from *The Original Water-color Paintings for The Birds of America*, published by American Heritage. Where there was a contradiction the latter book was used.

BIRDS OF AMERICA

Elephant Folio Editions

Plate		Havell Price	Bien Price	Bien Plate Number	Where Painted and Date	Artist Working on Background
1	Wild Turkey Cock	$40,000	$15,000	287	Beech Woods Plantation, La., West Feliciana Parish, 1825	Joseph Mason
2	Yellow-billed Cuckoo	3,500	2,000	275	Louisiana, 1821 or 1822	Joseph Mason
3	Prothonotary Warbler	2,250			Louisiana, 1821	Joseph Mason
4	Purple Finch	1,850	350	196	West Feliciana, La., 1825	
5	Bonaparte Flycatcher	2,250	350	73	Cypress Swamp near Bayou Sarah, 1821	Joseph Mason
6	Great American Hen	27,500			West Feliciana, La., 1825	
7	Purple Grackle	3,750	2,000	221	Louisiana, 1825	
8	White Throated Sparrow	2,000	350	191	Natchez, Miss., 1822	Joesph Mason
9	Selby's Flycatcher	1,750	350	71	Oakley, La., 1821	Joseph Mason
10	Brown Lark	1,500	275	151	New Orleans, La., Feb. 21, 1821	
11	Bird of Washington	6,500			New Orleans, 1822	
12	Baltimore Oriole	9,000	2,750	217	Louisiana, 1822 and later	Joseph Mason
13	Snow Bird	1,500			Louisiana, 1822	Joseph Mason
14	Prairie Warbler	1,750			Bayou Sarah, La., 1821	Joseph Mason
15	Blue Yellow-backed Warbler	2,000			Louisiana, 1821	Joseph Mason
16	Great-footed Hawk	5,500	2,000	20	Miss. River, La., Dec. 26, 1820	
17	Carolina Turtle Dove	12,500			Louisiana, 1825	
18	Bewick's Wren	1,750	300	118	Oakley Plantation, La., 1821	Joseph Mason
19	Louisiana Water Thrush	2,000			Bayou Sarah, 1821	Joseph Mason

Plate		Havell Price	Bien Price	Bien Plate Number	Where Painted and Date	Artist Working on Background
20	Blue Winged Yellow Warbler	$2,500			Louisiana, 1822	Joseph Mason
21	Mocking Bird	12,500	$2,750	138	Oakley, 1821, and Beech Woods, 1825	
22	Purple Martin	3,500	1,850	45	Louisiana or Mississippi, 1822	Joseph Mason
23	Maryland Yellow Throat	2,000			Louisiana, 1821	Joseph Mason
24	Roscoe's Yellow Throat	1,500			Bayou Sarah, La., 1821	Joseph Mason
25	Song Sparrow	1,750	300	189	Penn., 1812 and later	
26	Carolina Parrot	18,500	3,500	278	Louisiana, 1825	
27	Red-headed Woodpecker	3,500			Oakley, 1821	
28	Solitary Flycatcher	1,750	300	239	Louisiana, 1822	Joseph Mason
29	Towhee Bunting	2,250	350	195	Natchez, Mississippi, 1822	Joseph Mason
30	Vigors Vireo	2,250			Mill Grove, Penn., 1812	
31	White Headed Eagle	9,500	2,250	14	Miss. River at Little Prairie, Nov. 24, 1820	
32	Black-billed Cuckoo	5,500			Louisiana, 1822	Joseph Mason
33	American Goldfinch	2,500			New York, 1824	
34	Worm-eating Warbler	1,850			Louisiana or Miss., 1822	Joseph Mason
35	Children's Warbler	1,750	300	88	Oakley Plantation, La., 1821	Joseph Mason
36	Stanley Hawk	5,500			Bird at Top—Louisiana, 1825; Bottom Bird in Phil., 1824	
37	Gold Winged Woodpecker	6,500	2,000	273	Louisiana, 1821 and later	Joseph Mason
38	Kentucky Warbler	1,750	350	74	Louisiana or Miss., 1822	Joseph Mason
39	Crested Titmouse	2,250	350	125	Louisiana or Miss., 1822	Joseph Mason
40	American Redstart	2,250			Louisiana, 1821	Joseph Mason
41	Ruffed Grouse	12,500	3,000	293	New York or Penn., 1824	Joseph Mason

No.	Bird				Location, Date	Artist
42	Orchard Oriole	5,000	2,000	219	Louisiana, 1822	Joseph Mason
43	Cedar Bird	3,500	350	246	Cincinnati, Ohio, 1820	Joseph Mason
44	Summer Red Bird	4,250			Bayou Sarah, La., 1821 and later	Joseph Mason
45	Traill's Flycatcher	1,500			Fort Lakonson, 1822	Joseph Mason
46	Barred Owl	7,500			Louisiana, 1821	
47	Ruby-throated Hummingbird	9,750	3,000	253	Louisiana, 1825	Joseph Mason
48	Cerulean Warbler	1,750	350	86	Louisiana or Miss., 1822	Joseph Mason
49	Blue-green Warbler	1,600			Louisiana, 1821	Joseph Mason
50	Magnolia Warbler	1,250			Louisiana, 1821	Joseph Mason
51	Red Tailed Hawk	5,500			Louisiana, 1821	
52	Chuck-will's Widow	4,250	1,850	7	Natchez, Miss., 1822	
53	Painted Bunting	3,750			New Orleans, La., 1821	Joseph Mason
54	Rice Bunting	2,250			Louisiana, 1822	Joseph Mason
55	Cuvier's Wren	1,750			Fatland Ford, Penn., 1812	
56	Red Shouldered Hawk	6,750			Louisiana, 1825	
57	Loggerhead Shrike	2,500			Louisiana, 1825	
58	Hermit Thrush	1,750	350	144	New Orleans, 1822 and later	Joseph Mason
59	Chestnut-sided Warbler	1,500			Penn., 1812	
60	Carbonated Warbler	1,750	350	109	Henderson, Ky., 1811 and later	
61	Great Horned Owl	8,500			Henderson, Ky., 1814 and later	
62	Passenger Pigeon	9,250			Pittsburgh, Penn., 1824	
63	White-Eyed Flycatcher	1,750	300	240	New Orleans, La., 1821	Joseph Mason
64	Swamp Sparrow	1,750			Bayou Sarah (Lucy's name used)	Lucy Audubon or Joseph Mason
65	Rathbone Warbler	1,900	350	89	Falls of The Ohio, 1808	Joseph Mason
66	Ivory Billed Woodpecker	14,000			Louisiana, 1825	
67	Red Winged Blackbird	3,750	1,250	216	Louisiana, 1822	Joseph Mason

Plate		Havell Price	Bien Price	Bien Plate Number	Where Painted and Date	Artist Working on Background
68	Republican Cliff Swallow	$1,750	$350	48	Cincinnati, 1820 and later	
69	Bay-breasted Warbler	1,750	350	80	Penn., 1812	
70	Henslow's Bunting	1,500	300	163	Cincinnati, Ohio, 1820	
71	Winter Hawk	5,500			Louisiana, 1822	
72	Swallow-tailed Hawk	6,500	2,000	18	Oakley Plantation, 1821	
73	Wood Thrush	1,750	350	144	Natchez, Miss., 1822	Joseph Mason
74	Indigo Bird	2,750			Louisiana, 1821	Joseph Mason
75	Le Petit Caporal	2,250			Penn., 1812	Joseph Mason
76	Virginian Partridge	17,500	3,500	289	Beech Woods, 1825	
77	Belted Kingfisher	9,750	1,850	255	Little Bayou Sarah, La., 1812 and later	
78	Great Carolina Wren	2,750	350	127	Louisiana or Miss., 1822	Joseph Mason
79	Tyrant Flycatcher	1,750	350	56	Natchez, Miss., 1822	Joseph Mason
80	Prairie Titlark	1,250	300	150	Louisiana, 1822	
81	Fish Hawk	18,500	2,750	288	Great Egg Harbor, New Jersey, 1829	
82	Whip-poor-will	4,500			Mickle Swamp, N.J., 1829	
83	House Wren	3,500	350	120	Fatland Ford, Penn.	
84	Blue-grey Flycatcher	1,750	350	70	New Orleans, La., 1821	Joseph Mason
85	Yellow-throated Warbler	1,750			Louisiana, 1821	
86	Black Warrior	3,500			Louisiana, 1829	
87	Florida Jay	5,750			New Orleans, 1829	
88	Autumnal Warbler	1,500			Great Pine Swamp, 1829	
89	Nashville Warbler	2,000	350	113	Kentucky	George Lehman
90	Black and White Creeper	1,500	350	114	West Feliciana, La.	

94

No.	Bird				Location/Date	Artist
91	Broadwinged Hawk	6,750			Female Done at Fatland Ford, 1812—Male—West Feliciana, La., 1825	George Lehman
92	Pigeon Hawk	4,500	1,210	21	Eastern, U.S.—1829	
93	Sea Side Finch	4,500	500	172	Great Egg Harbor, 1829	
94	Bay-winged Bunting	2,250	350	159	Great Egg Harbor, 1829	
95	Blue-eyed Yellow Warbler	1,750	350	89	Natchez, 1822	Joseph Mason
96	Columbia Jay	6,500			Unknown	
97	Mottled Owl	7,500			New Jersey, 1829	
98	Marsh Wren	1,500	350	123	New Jersey, 1829	
99	Cow Bunting	1,250			Philadelphia, Pa., 1824	
100	White Bellied Swallow	1,500	300	46	Philadelphia, Pa., 1824	
	VOL. II					
101	Raven	5,750		231	Penn., 1829—Great Pine Forest	George Lehman
102	Blue Jay	12,500	3,000		Beech Woods, Feliciana, La., 1825	
103	Canada Warbler	2,000	350	72	Great Pine Forest, 1829	
104	Chipping Sparrow	1,500	300	165	Louisiana, 1821	Joseph Mason
105	Red Breasted Nuthatch	1,500			Great Pine Forest, Penn., 1829	
106	Black Vulture	3,500	1,500	3	Beech Grove, West Feliciana, La., 1829	
107	Canada Jay	6,500			State of Maine, 1829	George Lehman
108	Fox Colored Sparrow	1,750			Eastern U. S., 1824	
109	Savannah Finch	1,750			New Orleans, 1821	
110	Hooded Warbler	1,500	350	71	Louisiana, 1821 and later	Joseph Mason
111	Pileated Woodpecker	15,000	3,500	257	Penn., 1829	Joseph Mason
112	Downy Woodpecker	4,750			Louisiana or Miss., 1822	Joseph Mason
113	Blue Bird	2,500			Louisiana, 1822	

Plate		Havell Price	Bien Price	Bien Plate Number	Where Painted and Date	Artist Working on Background
114	White-crowned Sparrow	$1,500	$350	192	Henderson, Ky., 1814	George Lehman
115	Wood Pewee	1,250	300	63	New Jersey, 1829	George Lehman
116	Ferruginous Thrush	6,500	2,500	141	East—1829	
117	Mississippi Kite	4,500			Oakley Plantation, La., 1821	
118	Warbling Flycatcher	2,500			New Jersey, 1829	
119	Yellow Throated Vireo	1,750	300	79	James Pirrie's Plantation, 1821	Joseph Mason
120	Pewit Flycatcher	1,500			Louisiana, 1825	
121	Snowy Owl	19,500			Unknown	
122	Blue Grosbeak	3,500	2,000	294	New Orleans, La., 1821 and later	George Lehman
123	Black and Yellow Warbler	2,500	350	96	Great Pine Swamp, 1829	
124	Green Black-capped Flycatcher	1,750	350	75	New Jersey, 1829	
125	Brown-headed Nuthatch	1,500			Louisiana, 1829	
126	White Headed Eagle	6,500			Eastern U.S., 1829	
127	Rose-breasted Grosbeak	4,500	1,850	205	Eastern U.S., 1829	
128	Cat Bird	2,250			Louisiana or Miss., 1822	Joseph Mason
129	Great Crested Flycatcher	1,750	350	57	Philadelphia, 1824	
130	Yellow-winged Sparrow	1,750			Penn., 1812	
131	American Robin	9,500			New Jersey, 1829	
132	Three Toed Woodpecker	3,000			Great Pine Forest, Penn., 1829	George Lehman
133	Black Poll Warbler	1,750			New Jersey, 1829	George Lehman
134	Hemlock Warbler	1,750			Great Pine Swamp, 1829	
135	Blackburnian Warbler	1,500			Penn., 1812	

No.	Name				Location	Artist
136	Meadowlark	11,500			New Jersey	George Lehman
137	Yellow Breasted Chat	3,750	1,250	244	New Jersey, 1829	George Lehman
138	Connecticut Warbler	2,000			New Jersey, 1829	
139	Field Sparrow	1,750	300	164	Great Egg Harbor	
140	Pine-creeping Warbler	1,500	300	82	Pirrie Plantation, La., 1821	Joseph Mason
141	Goshawk	4,250			Henderson, Ky., Great Pine Forest, Penn., and Feliciana, La.	
142	American Sparrow Hawk	4,500		22	Eastern U.S., 1829	
143	Golden-crowned Thrush	1,750			New Jersey, 1829	
144	Small Green-crested Flycatcher	1,500	300	62	New Jersey, 1829	
145	Yellow Red-Poll Warbler	1,500	300	90	Bayou Lafourche, La., 1821	Joseph Mason
146	Fish Crow	4,500	1,850	226	New Orleans, La., 1821	
147	Night Hawk	3,500	1,850	43	New Jersey, 1829	
148	Pine Swamp Warbler	1,500			Great Pine Swamp, Penn., 1829	
149	Sharp-tailed Finch	1,750	350	174	New Jersey, 1829	Joseph Mason
150	Red-eyed Vireo	1,500	300	243	Louisiana or Miss., 1822	
151	Turkey Buzzard	3,750			Louisiana or Miss., 1822	
152	White-breasted Nuthatch	2,500			Louisiana or Miss., 1822	
153	Yellow Crown Warbler	1,750			Penn., 1812	
154	Tennessee Warbler	1,750			Louisiana, 1821	Joseph Mason
155	Black-throated Blue Warbler	1,750	300	95		
156	American Crow	6,750	2,750	225	Eastern U. S., 1829	George Lehman
157	Rusty Grackle	2,750	1,500	222	Louisiana	
158	American Swift	1,500	300	44	Saint Francisville, La.	
159	Cardinal	6,500			Louisiana or Miss., 1822	Joseph Mason

Plate		Havell Price	Bien Price	Bien Plate Number	Where Painted and Date	Artist Working on Background
160	Black-capped Titmouse	$1,750	$350	127	New Orleans, La., 1820	Joseph Mason
161	Caracara Eagle	6,500			St. Augustine, Florida, 1831	
162	Zenaida Dove	6,500			Florida Keys, 1832	George Lehman
163	Palm Warbler	1,750	350	90	St. Augustine, 1831-32	George Lehman
164	Tawny Thrush	1,750			Maine, 1832	Maria Martin
165	Bachman's Finch	1,750			Charleston, S. C., 1832	
166	Rough-legged Falcon	4,750			New Jersey, 1832	George Lehman
167	Key West Dove	6,500			Key West, Florida, 1832	Maria Martin
168	Fork-tailed Flycatcher	4,250	350	53	Camden, N.J., 1832	George Lehman
169	Mangrove Cuckoo	2,250			Key West, 1832	George Lehman
170	Gray Tyrant	1,950	350	55	Florida Keys, 1832	
171	Barn Owl	12,500	3,500	34	New Jersey, 1832	George Lehman
172	Blue-headed Pigeon	3,500			Key West, 1832	
173	Barn Swallow	2,500	350	48	New Jersey, 1832	
174	Olive-sided Flycatcher	1,750	350	58	Boston, Mass., 1832	
175	Marsh Wren	1,750	350	124	Boston, Mass., 1832	
176	Spotted Grouse	7,500			Maine, 1832	
177	White-crowned Pigeon	6,750	2,500		Indian Key, Florida, 1832	George Lehman
178	Orange Crowned Warbler	1,500			Eastern Florida, 1832	George Lehman
179	Wood Wren	1,750	350	119	Maine, 1832	John Audubon
180	Pine Finch	1,500			New Brunswick, 1832	
181	Golden Eagle	8,500			Boston, Mass., 1833	
182	Ground Dove	6,500			Charleston, S. C., 1831	George Lehman
183	Golden Crested Wren	1,500	350	132	Charleston, S. C., 1831	George Lehman
184	Mangrove Humming Bird	3,500	350	251	Charleston, S. C.	Maria Martin
185	Bachman's Warbler	2,750	350	108	Labrador, 1833	Maria Martin

No.	Species				Location	Artist
186	Pinnated Grouse	8,500			Unknown	George Lehman
187	Boat-tailed Grackle	4,500	2,500	296	Charleston, S. C., 1832	John Woodhouse Audubon
188	Tree Sparrow	1,500		220	Boston	
189	Snow Bunting	1,500			Boston, Mass., 1833	Joseph Mason
190	Yellow-bellied Woodpecker	2,250			Louisiana, 1822	
191	Willow Grouse	6,500			Labrador, 1833	
192	Great American Shrike	2,750			Boston, Mass., 1833	
193	Lincoln Finch	2,750	350	177	Labrador, 1833	
194	Hudsonian Titmouse	1,750	350	128	Labrador, 1833	
195	Ruby Crowned Wren	1,750	350	133	Labrador, 1833	
196	Labrador Falcon	3,750			Labrador, 1833	
197	American Crossbill	2,500	1,250	200	Maine, 1832	Maria Martin
198	Worm Eating Warbler	1,500	300	104	Charleston, S. C., 1832 (Painted by John Audubon)	
199	Little Owl	2,750			Boston, Mass., 1833	
200	Shore Lark	1,500			Labrador, 1833	
	VOL. III					
201	Canada Goose	25,000			Boston, Mass., 1833	
202	Red-throated Diver	7,500			Labrador, 1833 and later	
203	Fresh Water Marsh Hen	3,500			New Orleans, La., 1821	
204	Salt Water Marsh Hen	3,500			Charleston, S. C., 1833-34	
205	Virginia Rail	3,000			Charleston, S. C., 1833-34	
206	Summer or Wood Duck	15,000	3,500	391	Louisiana, 1821 and later	
207	Booby Gannet	3,750			Florida Keys, 1832	George Lehman
208	Esquimaux Curlew	2,250	350	357	Labrador, 1833	
209	Wilson's Plover	1,750			Florida, 1832	
210	Least Bittern	3,500			Philadelphia, 1832	
211	Great Blue Heron	35,000			Louisiana, 1821 and later	

Plate		Havell Price	Bien Price	Bien Plate Number	Where Painted and Date	Artist Working on Background
212	Common Gull	$3,000			Boston, 1832	
213	Puffin	5,250	$350	454	Labrador, 1833	
214	Razor Bill	1,500	300	466	Labrador, 1833	
215	Hyperborean Phalarope	1,500			Atlantic Coast, 1832	
216	Wood Ibis	19,500			Louisiana, 1821	George Lehman
217	Louisiana Heron	27,500			Florida, 1832	
218	Foolish Guillemot	1,500			Labrador, 1833	
219	Black Guillemot	1,750			State of Maine, 1833	
220	Piping Plover	1,500			Gulf of St. Lawrence, 1833	
221	Mallard Duck	25,000	3,500	385	Louisiana or Miss., 1821-1825	
222	White Ibis	12,500			Louisiana or Miss., 1821-1825	
223	Pied Oyster Catcher	2,500			Louisiana, 1821	
224	Kittiwake Gull	2,500			Boston, 1833	
225	Kildeer Plover	2,500			Bayou Sarah, La., 1825	
226	Whooping Crane	22,500			New Orleans, 1821-22	
227	Pin-tailed Duck	9,500			New Orleans, 1822	Victor Audubon
228	American Green Winged Teal	6,500			New Orleans, 1822	
229	Scaup Duck	5,750	1,500	397	Maine, 1833	
230	Ruddy Plover	2,250			England, 1834	
231	Long-billed Curlew	27,500			Charleston, S. C., 1831	George Lehman
232	Hooded Merganser	7,500			New Orleans, La., 1821	
233	Sora or Rail	2,500			New Orleans, La., 1821 and later	
234	Tufted Duck	5,750	1,500	398	New Orleans, 1821	
235	Sooty Tern	1,750			Dry Tortugas Islands, 1832	

No.	Name			Location	Artist
236	Night Heron	15,000		363	Charleston, S. C., 1832	George Lehman
237	Great Esquimaux Curlew	3,500			Louisiana, 1821	
238	Great Marbled Godwit	3,500	1,250	353	Louisiana, 1821 and later	
239	American Coot	3,500			East Florida, 1831	George Lehman
240	Roseate Tern	3,500			Indian Key, Florida, 1832	
241	Black-backed Gull	3,500			Northern Atlantic Coast, 1832	
242	Snowy Heron	25,000			Charleston, S. C.	George Lehman
243	American Snipe	3,750			Charleston, S. C., 1832	George Lehman
244	Common Gallinule	1,750			New Orleans, La., 1821	
245	Uria Brunnichi	1,500			Boston, 1833	
246	Eider Duck	12,500	2,500	405	Maine, 1833	
247	Velvet Duck	4,000			Maine, 1833	
248	American Pied Bill Dobchick	2,750			Louisiana, 1821 and later	
249	Tufted Auk	3,500			England, 1834-35	
250	Arctic Tern	2,750	350	434	Labrador, 1833	
251	Brown Pelican	27,500	3,500	423	Florida Keys, 1832	George Lehman
252	Florida Cormorant	4,500			Florida Keys, 1832	
253	Jager	1,500			Labrador, 1833	
254	Wilson's Phalarope	1,750			Northern Atlantic Coast, 1832-33	
255	Red Phalarope	1,750			London, 1835	
256	Purple Heron	17,500	2,250	371	Florida, 1832	
257	Double Crested Cormorant	3,000			Labrador, 1833	
258	Hudsonian Godwit	2,250			England, 1835	
259	Horned Grebe	2,250			Charleston, S. C., 1833-34	
260	Fork-tail Petrel	1,500			Newfoundland, 1831 and later	
261	Whooping Crane	19,500			Boston, 1832-33	
262	Tropic Bird	5,500			East Coast, 1832-35	
263	Pigmy Curlew	1,750	300	333	Atlantic Coast, 1832-34	

Plate		Havell Price	Bien Price	Bien Plate Number	Where Painted and Date	Artist Working on Background
264	Fulmar Petrel	$1,750			Unknown	
265	Buff Breasted Sandpiper	1,750	$300	331	Great Britain, 1835	
266	Common Cormorant	5,500			Labrador, 1833	
267	Arctic Yager	3,500			Great Britain, 1835	
268	American Woodcock	6,500			Atlantic Coast, 1832-34	
269	Greenshank	3,500	350	346	England, 1835	George Lehman
270	Stormy Petrel	1,250			On Board Ship Delos, 1826	
271	Frigate Pelican	7,500			Florida Keys, 1832	
272	Richardson's Jager	2,250			England, 1834	
273	Cayenne Tern	3,500			Key West, 1832	
274	Semipalmated Snipe	3,500			Atlantic Coast, 1832-34	
275	Noddy Tern	2,250			Noddy Key Island, 1832	
276	King Duck	7,500			Boston, 1832-33	
277	Hutchin's Goose	6,500			Great Britain, 1834-35	
278	Schinz Sandpiper	1,500			St. Augustine, Fla., 1831	George Lehman
279	Sandwich Tern	3,500	350	434	Florida Keys, 1832	
280	Black Tern	1,750			England, 1835	
281	Great White Heron	25,000	3,500	368	Key West, Florida, 1832	George Lehman
282	White Winged Silvery Gull	3,000			North Atlantic Coast, 1832-33	
283	Wandering Shearwater	1,750			Labrador, 1833	
284	Purple Sandpiper	1,500			Atlantic Coast, 1832-33 (John assisted)	
285	Fork-tailed Gull	1,750			England, 1835	
286	White-fronted Goose	12,500	3,500	380	Northern Atlantic Coast, 1832-33	

287	Ivory Gull	3,500		Great Britain, 1835	George Lehman
288	Yellow Shank	4,500	350	Charleston, S. C., 1832	
289	Solitary Sandpiper	2,250	300	Louisiana, 1825 and later	
290	Red-backed Sandpiper	1,750	300	Great Britain, 1835	
291	Herring Gull	5,750		St. Augustine, Fla., 1831 (Lehman painted lower one)	George Lehman
292	Crested Grebe	4,500	1,250	Great Britain, 1835	
293	Large-billed Puffin	3,000		England, 1834-35	
294	Pectoral Sandpiper	1,750	300	Maine, 1832	
295	Manks Shearwater	1,750		St. Georges, Newfoundland	Victor Audubon
296	Barnacle Goose	6,500		England, 1834-36	
297	Harlequin Duck	5,500		Unknown	
298	Red-necked Grebe	2,500		Boston, Mass., 1832-33	Victor Audubon
299	Dusky Petrel	1,500		Gulf of Mexico, 1826	
300	Golden Plover	1,500		New Orleans, La., 1821	
	VOL. IV				
301	Canvas-backed Duck	22,500	3,500	Baltimore and Louisiana, 1834 and 1821	
302	Dusky Duck	9,500	2,500	Atlantic Coast, 1832-34	
303	Bartram's Sandpiper	2,500		Louisiana, 1825	
304	Turnstone	2,250		Philadelphia, 1824	
305	Purple Gallinule	3,750		Louisiana, 1822	
306	Great Northern Diver	9,500		Labrador, 1833	
307	Blue Crane	17,500	3,500	New Orleans, La., 1821	George Lehman
308	Tell-Tale Godwit	2,500		Florida, 1832	George Lehman
309	Great Tern	2,500		Unknown	
310	Spotted Sandpiper	2,750	350	Bayou Sarah, La., 1821	
311	American White Pelican	27,500		Florida, 1831-32—unknown	George Lehman
312	Long-tailed Duck	7,500		Atlantic Coast, 1832-33	Victor Audubon

Plate		Havell Price	Bien Price	Bien Plate Number	Where Painted and Date	Artist Working on Background
313	Blue-winged Teal	$6,500			New Orleans, La., 1822 and later	
314	Black-headed Gull	2,250			Great Egg Harbor, New Jersey, 1829	
315	Red-breasted Sandpiper	1,750			Louisiana, 1821 and later	
316	Black-bellied Darter	6,500			New Orleans, La., 1822	
317	Black or Surf Duck	4,500			Labrador, 1833	
318	American Avocet	3,750			New Orleans, La., 1821	
319	Lesser Tern	3,500			Louisiana, 1821 and later	
320	Little Sandpiper	2,500	$350	331	Bayou Sarah, La., 1825	
321	Roseate Spoonbill	30,000			Florida, 1831-32	George Lehman
322	Red-headed Duck	8,750	2,500	396	Boston, Mass., 1832-35	
323	Black Skimmer	5,500	750	428	New Orleans, La., 1821	
324	Bonaparte Gull	3,500			Louisiana, 1821 and elsewhere, 1830	
325	Buffel-headed Duck	6,500			Maine, 1833	
326	Gannet	6,500			Gulf of St. Lawrence, 1833	
327	Shoveller Duck	12,500			Eastern U.S., 1832	
328	Long-legged Avocet	3,000			New Orleans, La., 1821	
329	Yellow-breasted Rail	1,500	300	308	New Orleans, La., 1821	
330	Ring Plover	1,500			Philadelphia, 1824	
331	American Merganser	8,500			Northern Atlantic Coast, 1832-33	
332	Pied Duck	5,500			Boston, Mass., 1832-33	
333	Green Heron	8,500	2,500	367	Louisiana, 1821-22	
334	Black Bellied Plover	1,500			Atlantic Coast, 1833 and Louisiana, 1822	

No.	Name				Location, Date	Attribution
335	Red Breasted Snipe	1,750			Atlantic Coast, 1832-33	
336	Yellow Crowned Heron	12,500	3,500	364	Charleston, S. C., 1831	Maria Martin
337	American Bittern	6,500			Atlantic Coast, 1832-33 (Attributed to John)	
338	Bemaculated Duck	6,500			New Orleans, La., 1822	
339	Little Auk	1,500			Northern Atlantic Coast, 1832-33	
340	Least Stormy Petrel	1,500			Unknown	
341	Great Auk	9,500	3,500	465	London, 1834-36	Victor Audubon
342	Golden Eye Duck	6,500			Atlantic Coast, 1832-34	
343	Ruddy Duck	7,500			New Orleans, La.	
344	Long-legged Sandpiper	1,750			Atlantic Coast, 1833	
345	American Widgeon	7,500			New Orleans, La., 1821	
346	Black-throated Diver	9,500			London	
347	Smew or White Nun	5,500	2,500	414	Great Britain, 1834-35	
348	Gadwall Duck	7,500	1,250	288	Atlantic Coast, 1832-34	
349	Least Water Hen	1,500	300	308	Philadelphia, Pa., 1836	
350	Rocky Mountain Plover	1,250			Philadelphia, Pa., 1836	
351	Great Cinereous Owl	8,500			England, 1834-36	
352	Black-Winged Hawk	5,500	2,500	16	Charleston, S. C., 1834	
353	Chestnut-backed Titmouse	2,500			Charleston, S. C., 1836	Maria Martin
354	Louisiana Tanager	4,500			Charleston, S. C., 1836-37	Maria Martin
355	MacGillivray's Finch	2,250	350	173	Charleston, S. C., 1833 (Attributed to John)	Maria Martin
356	Marsh Hawk	6,500			Mississippi River, 1820	
357	American Magpie	3,750			England, 1835-36	
358	Pine Grosbeak	1,750	350	199	Charleston, S. C., 1833-34	
359	Arkansas Flycatcher	2,500	350	54	Charleston, S. C., 1836-37	Victor Audubon

Plate	Havell Price	Bien Price	Bien Plate Number	Where Painted and Date	Artist Working on Background
360	$2,500	$350	121 & 116	Miss. River, 1820; Maine, 1833; Charleston, 1836	
361	6,500			Charleston, S. C., 1836-37	Victor Audubon
362	4,500			Charleston, S. C., 1836-37	Maria Martin
363	1,750	350	245	Great Britain, 1835	
364	1,750			Labrador, 1833	Victor Audubon
365	1,750			Labrador, 1833	
366	22,500	3,500	19	Great Britain, 1835-36	Maria Martin
367	5,500			Charleston, S. C., 1836-37	Victor Audubon
368	4,500			Great Britain, 1836-37	Maria Martin
369	2,750			Philadelphia, 1836	Victor Audubon
370	1,500			Charleston, S. C., 1836-37	Victor Audubon
371	9,500			Charleston, S. C., 1836-37	
372	5,750			Charleston, S. C., 1836-37	
373	2,250			Charleston, S. C., 1836-37	Maria Martin
374	2,500			Henderson, Ky., 1812 and Cincinnati, Ohio, 1820, Charleston later	
375	1,750			Labrador, 1833	
376	17,500			New Orleans, La., 1822	
377	5,500			Charleston, S. C., 1836-37	
378	2,500			Charleston, S. C., 1836-37	
379	6,750			Charleston, S. C., 1836-37	Maria Martin
380	3,500			Bangor, Maine, 1832	

Plate 360 — Winter Wren
Plate 361 — Dusky Grouse
Plate 362 — Yellow-billed Magpie
Plate 363 — Bohemian Chatterer
Plate 364 — White-winged Crossbill
Plate 365 — Lapland Longspur
Plate 366 — Iceland Falcon
Plate 367 — Band-tailed Pigeon
Plate 368 — Rock Grouse
Plate 369 — Mountain Mocking Bird
Plate 370 — American Water Ouzel
Plate 371 — Cock of the Plains
Plate 372 — Common Buzzard
Plate 373 — Evening Grosbeak
Plate 374 — Sharp-shinned Hawk
Plate 375 — Lesser Redpoll
Plate 376 — Trumpeter Swan
Plate 377 — Scolopacius Courlan
Plate 378 — Hawk Owl
Plate 379 — Ruff-necked Humming Bird
Plate 380 — Tengmalm's Owl

No.	Bird	Count		Place and Date	Artist
381	Snow Goose	9,500		Boston, 1832 and later	Victor Audubon
382	Sharp-tailed Grouse	6,500		Charleston, S. C., 1836-37	
383	Long-eared Owl	3,500		Penn., 1829	
384	Black-throated Bunting	1,750		Natchez, Miss., 1822	
385	Bank Swallow	1,750		Philadelphia, 1824	
386	White Heron	22,500		Charleston, S. C., 1832	
387	Glossy Ibis	8,500	2,750	Charleston, S. C., 1836-37	
388	Nuttall's Starling	2,250		Charleston, S. C., 1836-37	
389	Red-cockaded Woodpecker	1,750		Oakley Plantation, 1821 and elsewhere, 1836	
390	Lark Finch	1,750	358	Charleston, S. C., 1836-37	Victor Audubon
391	Brant Goose	6,500		Philadelphia, 1824	
392	Louisiana Hawk	5,500		London, 1837	
393	Townsend's Warbler	2,500		Charleston, S. C., 1836-37	Maria Martin
394	Chestnut Colored Finch	2,500		Charleston, S. C., 1836-37	Maria Martin
395	Audubon's Warbler	2,250		Charleston, S. C., 1836-37	Maria Martin
396	Burgomaster Gull	3,750		England, 1836	
397	Scarlet Ibis	9,500		England, 1837	
398	Lazuli Finch	2,250		Charleston, S. C., 1836-37	Maria Martin
399	Black-throated Green Warbler	2,250		Charleston, S. C., 1836-37	
400	Arkansas Siskin	1,750		Unknown	
401	Red Breasted Merganser	9,500		Charleston, S. C., 1833-34	
402	Black Throated Guillemot	3,500		London, 1837	
403	Golden Eye Duck	3,500		London, 1838	
404	Eared Grebe	2,750		London, 1838	
405	Semipalmated Sandpiper	1,750	300 / 336	London, 1838	
406	Trumpeter Swan	37,500		(Use author)	
407	Dusky Albatross	2,750		London, 1838	
408	American Scoter Duck	3,500		London, 1838	

Plate		Havell Price	Bien Price	Bien Plate Number	Where Painted and Date	Artist Working on Background
409	Havell's Tern	$2,750			London, 1838	
410	Marsh Tern	2,750			London, 1838	
411	Common American Swan	27,500			Miss. River Delta, 1837	
412	Violet Green Cormorant	3,250			London, 1838	
413	California Partridge	4,500			London, 1837	
414	Golden-winged Warbler	1,750			Charleston, S. C., 1836-37	Maria Martin
415	Brown Creeper	1,750			London	
416	Hairy Woodpecker	9,500			Charleston, S. C., 1836-37	Maria Martin
417	Maria's Woodpecker	7,500			London, 1838	
418	American Ptarmigan	3,500			London, 1838	
419	Little Tawny Thrush	1,750			London, 1838	
420	Prairie Starling	1,750			London, 1838	
421	Brown Pelican	27,500			New Orleans, La., 1821	Victor Audubon
422	Rough-legged Falcon	4,500			England, 1838	
423	Plumed Partridge	4,500			London, 1838	
424	Lazuli Finch	2,250			London, 1838	
425	Columbian Humming Bird	4,500	$350	252	London, 1838	Maria Martin
426	California Vulture	7,500			London, 1838	
427	White-legged Oyster Catcher	4,500			London, 1838	
428	Townsend's Sandpiper	1,750			London, 1838	
429	Western Duck	4,500			England, 1838	
430	Slender-billed Guillemot	1,250			London, 1838	
431	American Flamingo	35,000	3,500	375	England, 1838	
432	Burrowing Owl	4,500			London, 1838	
433	Bullock's Oriole	1,750			London, 1838	
434	Little Tyrant Flycatcher	1,750			London, 1838	
435	Columbia Water Ouzel	1,750			London, 1838	

THE VIVIPAROUS QUADRUPEDS
OF NORTH AMERICA
Imperial Folio Price List

Plate
No.

1	Common American Wild Cat	$3,500
2	Woodchuck	1,250
3	Townsend's Rocky Mountain Hare	1,500
4	Florida Rat	375
5	Richardson's Columbian Squirrel	900
6	American Red-Fox	2,250
7	Carolina Grey Squirrel	1,500
8	Chipping Squirrel	1,500
9	Parry's Marmot Squirrel	550
10	Common American Shrew Mole	295
11	Northern Hare, Summer	1,500
12	Northern Hare	1,500
13	Musk-Rat, Musquash	750
14	Fremont's Squirrel	1,500
15	Rocky Mountain Flying Squirrel	1,500
16	Canada Lynx	3,000
17	Cat Squirrel	1,500
18	Marsh Hare	1,250
19	Douglass Squirrel	1,250
20	Townsend's Ground Squirrel	750
21	Grey Fox	4,500
22	Grey Rabbit	1,850
23	Black Rat	350
24	Four-Striped Ground Squirrel	950
25	Downy Squirrel	1,250
26	The Wolverine	1,850
27	Long Haired Squirrel	1,500
28	Common Flying Squirrel	1,850
29	Rocky Mountain Neotoma	450
30	Cotton Rat	475
31	Collared Peccary	4,500

Bibliography

Arthur, Stanley Clisby. *Audubon: An Intimate Life of The American Woodsman.* New Orleans: Harmanson, 1937.

"Audubon in Liverpool." In *Outlook.* Liverpool, England: University of Liverpool, 1962.

Audubon, John James. *The Birds of America.* New York: Macmillan Co., 1946.

Audubon, John James. *The Birds of America from Original Drawings.* London: John James Audubon, 1827-30.

Audubon, John James. *The Birds of America, From Drawings Made in the U.S. and Their Territories.* New York: V. G. Audubon, 1859.

Audubon, John James. *Delineations of American Scenery and Character.* New York: G. A. Baker and Co., 1926.

Audubon, John James. *The Original Water-color Paintings for The Birds of America.* New York: America Heritage Publication Co., 1966.

Audubon, John James. *Ornithological Biography.* Edinburgh, 1831.

Audubon, Mrs. J. J. *The Life of John James Audubon: The Naturalist.* New York: Putnam, 1869.

Audubon, Maria R., ed. *Audubon and His Journals.* New York: Dover Publications, 1960.

Audubon, John James and Bachman, John. *The Quadrupeds of North America.* New York: Ludwig and Co., 1849.

Audubon Watercolors and Drawings. Utica: Munson-Williams-Proctor Institute, and New York: The Pierpont Morgan Library, 1965.

Bradford, Mary F. *Audubon*. New Orleans: L. Graham & Son, 1897.

Buchanan, Robert W. *The Life and Adventures of John James Audubon: The Naturalist*. London: Sampson Low, 1869.

Buckner, Hollingsworth. *Her Garden Was Her Delight*. New York: Macmillan Co., 1962.

Burroughs, John. *John James Audubon*. Boston: Small, Maynard, & Co., 1902.

Coffin, Annie R. "Marie Martin." In *Art Quarterly*. Autumn, 1960.

Dwight, Edward H. "Audubon The Artist." In *Audubon Magazine*. January-February 1963.

Fisher, George Clyde. *The Life of Audubon*. New York: Harper, 1947.

Ford, Alice. *Audubon's Animals: The Quadrupeds of North America*. New York: Studio Publications, 1951.

Ford, Alice. *Audubon's Butterflies, Moths, and Other Studies*. New York: Studio Publications, 1952.

Ford, Alice. *John James Audubon*. Norman: University of Oklahoma Press, 1964.

Ford, Alice, ed. *Audubon By Himself*. Garden City, New York: The Natural History Press, 1969.

Freeland, W. O. *A Survey Exhibition in Memory of Maria Martin*. Columbia, South Carolina: Columbia Museum of Art, 1964.

Fries, Waldemar H. *Double Elephant Folio: The Story of Audubon's Birds of America*. Chicago: American Library Association, 1973.

Gifford, Dr. G. Edmund. "Audubon's Massachusetts Artist: Isaac Sprague." In *Massachusetts Audubon Newsletter*. Vol. 14, no. 5 (1975).

Griscome, Ludlow. *Audubon's Birds Of America*. New York: Macmillan, 1950.

Groce, George C., and Wallace, David P. *The New York His-torical Society's Directory of Artists in America.* New Haven: Yale University Press; London: Oxford University Press, 1957.

Hardy, Eric. "When Audubon Visited Liverpool." In *The Naturalist.* Liverpool: September, 1930.

Hanaburgh, E. F. *Audubon's "Birds of America."* Buchanan, New York: 1941.

Herrick, Francis Hobart. *Audubon: The Naturalist.* New York and London: D. Appleton & Co., 1917.

Louisiana State Museum, Friends of The Cabildo. *Audubon In Louisiana.* New Orleans: 1966.

Murphy, Robert Cushman. "John James: An Evaluation of The Man and His Works." In *New York Historical Quarterly.* 39-40 (1955-56).

Rice, Howard C. Jr. "A Study of the Successive Stages and Techniques of Audubon's Elephant Folio Engravings." In *Princeton University Library Chronicle.* 21, nos. 1-2 (1959-60).

Rourke, Constance. *Audubon.* New York: Harcourt, Brace & Co., 1936.

Unpublished Sources

Bachman, Maria Martin. Watercolor drawings and notes. Collection in the Charleston Museum, Charleston, South Carolina.

Bannon, Lois E. Monograph of art works of John James Audubon. In Louisiana State University Archives, Baton Rouge, Louisiana.

Collection of Audubon Letters. In Houghton Library, Harvard University, Cambridge, Massachusetts.

Recorded auction and other sales prices of Audubon prints and books from 1966-1976. In the Taylor Clark Galleries, Baton Rouge, Louisiana.

Sprague, Isaac. Biography of Isaac Sprague. In the Boston Museum of Fine Arts, Boston, Massachusetts.

Sprague, Isaac. Diary by Isaac Sprague. In the Boston Athenaeum, Boston, Massachusetts.

Index

Addendum
Notes and Prices as of 1984

Interest in Audubon's work has not diminished, nor have prices. A complete Havell double-elephant folio set of *The Birds Of America* sold for $1,540,000 at a February 1984 auction. A complete set of the octavo *Birds* is selling for $9,500 to $15,000 depending on the condition of the paper, the bindings, and the edition. The individual octavo bird prints are selling for $50 to $500 for the first edition Turkey. The four volume Amsterdam edition of *The Birds,* a reproduction of the double-elephant folio Havell edition, was published in 1971. A bound set sells today for $35,000, an unbound set for $25,000. A rule of thumb is that an individual Amsterdam print sells for about one-tenth of the same Havell print.

The February 1984 auction prices for complete bound sets of imperial editions of *The Viviparous Quadrupeds of North America* were $87,490 and $51,630. A complete set of octavo *Quadrupeds* is selling for $2,000 to $3,500 for the first edition and $1,500 to $2,500 for later editions depending on the condition of the pages and the binding. The individual prints sell for $50 to $350 depending on the animal and the condition of the print. In 1980 Volair Limited published copies of complete octavo first editions of *The Birds* and *The Quadrupeds* (see pages 47, 48, and 74).

Since the first edition of this book was published, two items have been called to our attention. One is the publication dates on the first edition octavo *Quadrupeds*. We have been sent information about sets of the octavo volumes that appear to be first editions with dates of 1851 (volumes 1 and 2) and 1854 (volume 3). This contradicts the information we gleaned from Herrick and Arthur's books. Unless many volumes can be compared, we cannot comment on this. The authors would welcome information from anyone who owns possible first edition *Quadrupeds* that are not dated as specified on page 76. The second item is the coloring method of the Lockwood octavo editions of both *The Birds* and *The Quadrupeds*. The ones we have seen appear to be hand-colored. It would be helpful if anyone having a Lockwood edition that appears not to be hand-colored would contact us so that we can review additional examples.

As this revised edition goes to press, the world is celebrating the two hundredth anniversary of Audubon's birth. Many special exhibits and publications have been planned. Additional reproductions of the famous prints may confuse the collector. However, most of the reproductions will be recognized by definite marks. For example, Southart-Parkway is planning a facsimile of some of the imperial folio *Quadrupeds*. They will be identified by a blind embossed seal. Others are planning to reproduce some of the birds in various sizes, including the elephant folio size. There is also a possibility that restrikes from a few of the original copper plates will be attempted. Collectors are reminded that the Havell edition is watermarked.

LOIS E. BANNON

NOTES ON QUADRUPED PRINTS

RECORD OF PURCHASES

Date	Plate No.	Place of Purchase	Cost